SPRINGBOARDS *for* TEACHING

ALL ABOARD!

Cross-Curricular Design and Technology Strategies and Activities

Written by
The Metropolitan Toronto School Board

Edited by Julie E. Czerneda

Trifolium Books Inc.
Toronto

Trifolium Books Inc.

238 Davenport Road, Suite 28
Toronto, Ontario, Canada M5R 1J6

The discussion of rubrics and their use in design and technology was contributed by Susan Baker-Proud, of the Waterloo Region Roman Catholic Separate School Board, adapted from her book, *Career Connections Series III Teacher Resource Bank* (published by Trifolium Books Inc., and Weigl Educational Publishers).

Any other activities or text features which did not appear in the publication *Springboards to Technology* were contributed by Julie Czerneda.

Care has been taken to trace ownership of copyright material contained in this book. The publishers will gladly receive any information that will enable them to rectify any reference or credit line in subsequent editions.

Special Note: This resource has been reviewed for bias and stereotyping.

Canadian Cataloguing in Publication Data

Main entry under title

All Aboard! Cross-Curricular Design and Technology Strategies & Activities

(Springboards for teaching series)

Includes bibliographical references.

ISBN 1-895579-86-4

1. Design, Industrial - Study and teaching (Elementary). 2. Technology - Study and teaching (Elementary). I. Rhodes, Sheila. II. Metropolitan Toronto Board of Education. III. Series.

LB 1594.S67 1996   372.3'58044   C96-931510-4

Project editor: Julie Czerneda
Design, layout: Roger Czerneda
Cover design: Blanche Hamil
Project coordinator: Diane Klim
Production coordinator: Francine Geraci
Graphics: Roger Czerneda

Printed and bound in Canada

10 9 8 7 6 5 4 3 2 1

Trifolium's books may be purchased in bulk for educational, business, or promotional use. For information, please write: Special Sales, Trifolium Books Inc., 238 Davenport Road, Suite 28, Toronto, Ontario, Canada M5R 1J6

This book's text stock contains more than 50% recycled paper.

Safety First!

Safety: The activities in this book are safe when carried out in an organized, structured setting. Please ensure you provide to your students specific information about the safety routines used in your school. It is, of course, critical to assess your students' level of responsibility in determining which materials and tools to allow them to use.

Note: If you are not completely familiar with the safety requirements for the use of specialized equipment, please consult with the appropriate specialty teacher(s) before allowing use by students. As well, please make sure that your students know where all the safety equipment is, and how to use it. The publisher and authors can accept no responsibility for any damage caused or sustained by use or misuse of ideas or materials mentioned in this book.

What's New?

If you would like to know about other Trifolium resources, please visit our Web Site at:

www.pubcouncil.ca/trifolium

Project Development Team

Project Manager

Sheila Rhodes, The Board of Education for the City of York

Writing Team Members

Lena Kozovski . . . . .East York Board of Education
Marilynn Pascale . . . . .The Board of Education for the City of York
Sheila Rhodes . . . . .The Board of Education for the City of York
Yvonne Simpson . . . . .North York Board of Education
Peter Williams . . . . .Toronto Board of Education

Advisory Board

Neil Bailey . . . . .North York Board of Education
Sheila Cutler . . . . .Etobicoke Board of Education
Norm Dale . . . . .The Board of Education for the City of York
Geoff Day . . . . .The Board of Education for the City of York
David Joyce . . . . .East York Board of Education
Allan Mawson . . . . .Scarborough Board of Education
Kathleen McCabe . . . . .The Board of Education for the City of York
Carol Munroe . . . . .East York Board of Education
Olga Panowyk . . . . .Toronto Board of Education,
Dick Roberts . . . . .Etobicoke Board of Education
Les Tankard . . . . .Scarborough Board of Education
Joe Hogan . . . . .Scarborough Board of Education
Joan Thompson . . . . .East York Board of Education

Field Test Teachers

East York Board of Education
Jane Ast   Beth Cuccia
Dorothy Irving   Sue Swain
North York Board of Education
Dawn Gillespie   Voula Lionlias
Jonathan Hatt   Kurt Metzler
Alan Lawrason   Sandra Stembridge
Steve Liebgott   Linda Wunch
Scarborough Board of Education
Stephen Gilchrist   Marian White
Liz Hall   Christine Whittich
Gary Hopson   Suzanne Witkin
Christine Howe
Toronto Board of Education
Georgina Kagianis   Jenny Megas
Katherine McKeowan   Peggy Williams
The Board of Education for the City of York
Tammy Clemmenson   Claire Keith
Gord Dove   Bev O'Brien

Acknowledgements

There are many models used for the design process. One that has proven to be very effective is the SPICE model (S=Situation; P=Problems/Possibilities; I= Investigations/Ideas; C= Choose/Construct; E=Evaluate). The SPICE model was created and developed by Geoff Day for teaching Design and Technology courses at the Faculty of Education, University of Toronto. It has been used, with Geoff's permission, in several forms in materials developed under the auspices of The Metropolitan School Board since 1989, and we thank him for its use in this book.

We also thank the writing team members, the advisory board, and the field test teachers for producing such a fine resource. We thank the many reviewers who gave us feedback during the preparation of this new edition, including: Bob Emptage, Doug Brandon, and Eric Sayle from the Simcoe Board of Education. Your enthusiasm and understanding of the needs of teachers and students were of immense help. Finally, we thank Julie and Roger Czerneda for their fine efforts in producing this new teaching and learning resource.

The Metropolitan Toronto School Board and Trifolium Books Inc.

Foreword

Children want to know about their world. They enjoy learning by doing. And they want to understand how things fit together. These are the foundations of the approach to cross-curricular learning presented to you in this book.

All Aboard! Cross-curricular Design and Technology Strategies and Activities is an updated and enhanced version of a breakthrough resource prepared by teachers of the The Metropolitan Toronto School Board, originally entitled *Springboards to Technology* (one of its major projects in which curriculum materials are developed co-operatively among the six public Area Boards of Education in the Metropolitan Toronto and The Metropolitan Toronto School Board). The original book came to be because educators were intent on helping students better understand the technology around them through problem-solving, creativity, and evaluation. The result was an acclaimed resource that was applicable across all curriculum.

We believe it will be apparent to you that *All Aboard! Cross-curricular Design and Technology Strategies and Activities* draws on the experience of technology educators, as well as subject specialists in all other curriculum areas. It shows how technology can be presented in every elementary school classroom, with the aim of linking all curriculum areas in a natural and cohesive manner. The real world nature of the topics lends itself perfectly to connecting with other teachers, parents, and the community.

In 1995 and in early 1996, Trifolium Books Inc. went to teachers who were using the original curriculum document (*Springboards to Technology*) to find out what they saw as key areas to improve and update in this excellent resource. The revisions and expansions our project editor, Julie Czerneda, has made to the original document in creating this new version, *All Aboard! Cross-curricular Design and Technology Strategies and Activities*, are based on the recommendations they provided, making a fine resource even better.

The Metropolitan Toronto School Board and Trifolium Books Inc. are pleased to provide this book for your own use, making the wonderful ideas and experiences of the curriculum writing team available to teachers and students in other jurisdictions. We are confident its use will greatly enhance student learning and skills development.

The Metropolitan Toronto School Board and Trifolium Books Inc.

Contents at a Glance

Features of this Book

There are several features of this book that we believe will be particularly helpful to you each time you use it.

Planning Sheets

In the appendix, you'll find reproducible *Planning Sheets*, covering all aspects of setting up and getting going in design and technology.

Wish Lists

In the appendix, you'll find reproducible lists of suitable tools, materials, and other resources.

Review of Construction Kits

Wondering which kit to use with a particular group of students? Check out the review of commonly purchased kits in the appendix.

Overview Charts

Each set of activities begins with a chart listing the project, recommended materials, and any special advance planning to consider such as scheduling library time. You'll also find optional ideas to enrich or extend your program.

Topic Webs

Webs are used throughout this book as a tool to help show interrelationships and to organize information.

Internet Ideas

There are pages of Internet addresses that you and your students can use as part of your exploration of technology, as well as ideas for research tied to many activities.

Computers and Other Information Technologies

While this book targets ready-to-use, inexpensive ways to achieve excellent results with your students, the option of using computers for design, control, and presentation work is presented where appropriate.

Links to the Community

There a numerous opportunities to link activities to the community, through field trips, classroom visitors, and student experiences.

New to Rubrics?

There is a section on using rubrics for authentic assessment that includes an activity for students to produce their own.

For Your Students

There are reproducible student pages for each featured activity, as well as general forms for self-, peer-, and group assessment, and project evaluation. You'll also find a *Safety Quiz* and *Contract* that will help you address safety issues with your students.

TEACHER SUPPORT SECTION

ALL ABOARD!

Welcome to the wonderful world of design and technology. Learning through doing excites, stimulates, and motivates children. There is no area of learning more firmly entrenched in this concept than design and technology.

Design and technology education is far more than a way of keeping students interested. As they progress through the activities, you'll see your students engage naturally in discussion and collaboration. They will consider others' needs and wants as they apply themselves to problems that are directly linked to the real world. Your students will benefit greatly from being exposed to the problem-solving method that is so integral to the design process. And finally, you'll be witness to the satisfaction and confidence your students will gain as they realize that there is no single right answer -- that a variety of worthwhile solutions is possible in any situation.

The title of this book focuses attention on the cross-curricular nature of design and technology. You will find that the design and technology activities in this book serve as an excellent way to link different curriculum areas, while at the same time making students more familiar with the technology around them and with the problem-solving design process.

By working through the activities in this book with your students, you will help clarify the technology students will encounter in their lives. You will enable your students to make and test propositions. As a result, we are confident they will develop a more complete understanding of their world.

TEACHING DESIGN AND TECHNOLOGY

Around the world, the significance and delivery of design and technology are being given fresh emphasis by educators. Some jurisdictions begin at the Junior Kindergarten level. In most, design and technology is studied by all students as part of the core curriculum from elementary to middle school. At this level, technology is used as a practical integrator for all subjects, in addition to treatment as a core subject.

You will find more detailed description of the concepts best suited to the different grades starting on page 19 in this book. Here is an overview:

Focus in the Kindergarten

In students' early years (Junior and Senior Kindergarten), the focus of any design and technology program should be to expand the knowledge of children and their world by:

○ the introduction and development of a technological awareness by integrating technological concepts into the comprehensive program;

○ enhancing and expanding the many experiences of a technological nature that currently exist for children inside and outside of school;

○ providing a learning environment that promotes growth and development in a variety of skills: practical, communication, reasoning, and interpersonal.

Focus in Grades 1 to 6

The program focus in Grades 1 to 6 should be to broaden and enhance the knowledge of children and their world by:

○ expanding the development of a technological awareness through the integration of technological concepts into the comprehensive program;

○ recognizing technological concepts (structures, materials, fabrication, mechanisms, power and energy, control, systems, function, aesthetics and ergonomics) in other subject areas and in various contexts: self, school, family, community, and the environment;

○ participating actively in a balanced program where technological concepts are integrated and identifiable;

○ the introduction to the use of a design procedure and a process of inquiry.

The area of design and technology inspires innovative thinking and creative perspectives. Its teaching is an interactive process that fosters children's intellectual and physical capabilities. They learn to explore and create. They delight in the power of their own thinking.

Helping Hand

You'll find a discussion on how the various technological concepts fit into grades K-6 starting on page 28.

Problem-solving in the Curriculum

Problem-solving is, of course, an extremely important skill. The design process is one form of creative problem-solving. The elements of design and technology lead to an endless assortment of solutions to the same problem and produce concrete results by which students can test their ideas. Design and technology revolves around the creative process of synthesis - students drawing on previously gained knowledge to develop new ideas.

This process takes time to develop. Young children require more guided activities. Group work is not as easily implemented in K-3 as in grades 4-6, but it will develop through continued application of this approach.

Any curriculum today must provide opportunities for students to work on simple problem-solving activities to help them in the design process. Divergent thinking is encouraged in this manner. Students learn to evaluate their ideas. There evolves a greater understanding of the social implications inherent in the processes of designing and creating.

Co-operation is a key element in problem-solving. Working in pairs or small groups, students are often able to develop new solutions they might not have considered working in isolation. The design process is beautifully suited to this collaborative approach.

Collaborative Work

Collaborative work, apart from stimulating creative thought, inventiveness, and the development of manipulative skills, involves students in activities that require co-operation, which fosters their social and communication skills. Working with others provides opportunities for students to appreciate the capabilities of others. Children with special talents come into their own. These learners get to show those talents that might otherwise have remained hidden. In addition, the teacher and students work together to negotiate learning outcomes. There can be a real exchange of perspectives and insights.

While developing solutions to problems, students form co-operative partnerships to identify and clarify problems. Through the clarification of roles within the group, students learn to build on the expertise of others. They learn to flow in and out of a variety of roles as expectations change. They arrive at consensus through the development of common goals. They must address certain problems in order to find an appropriate solution. All students in the group, and in the larger class, appreciate the need to share materials and ideas. This exchange helps students develop the communication skills required to explain their concepts and approaches.

The spirit of design and technology relies on the development of collaborative inquiry. All members of the group share an investment in the success of the final project, and all of them experience the full sense of exploration and celebration.

When young children are encouraged to become risk-takers, they are more capable of addressing issues related to the diverse nature of our ever-changing world.

One of the delightful consequences of the problem-solving approach used in design and technology is that as students generate a variety of solutions to a given problem, they come to view difficulties as new opportunities rather than disappointments.

GETTING STARTED: YOUR CLASSROOM

This is where you will find out what kinds of advance planning and equipment you'll need if you have not tried doing design and technology activities in your class before. There are also helpful tips and suggestions throughout this section for your future reference.

Your success, as in any unit you teach, depends on careful planning. While all of the activities in this book can be done with simple materials and basic skills, the quality of the experience for both you and the students will be enhanced by the little details that you arrange ahead of time. Here is a list of suggestions that other teachers have found helpful.

General Comments

O Choose activities that take the interests and abilities of the learners into account.

O Work from the experiences of the children to build learning activities that ensure appropriate outcomes are covered.

O Generate new activities that provide opportunities for children to explore and experiment from the context of a topic-based unit.

O Considering health and safety factors.

O Arrange time, space, and resources.

O Obtain parental support and community involvement.

O Prepare a series of sequential steps for the theme and each activity.

O Plan evaluation and assessment strategies that are meaningful to your students.

O Be prepared to adapt to the everyday aspects of school life.

Expected Learning Outcomes

It is important to know what areas you want to cover while working on a particular topic. Consider areas of the traditional curriculum that could be linked naturally. Decide which design and technology expectations are to be addressed. A detailed description of the links between design and technology and other areas of curriculum is provided in the next section of this book, entitled *Content and Curriculum*, starting on page 19.

Confirm that students have the necessary background knowledge and skills required for this topic. If they don't, decide how they are going to acquire them. And last, but not least, you will want to make sure that you have some background knowledge to assist students. This is not difficult today, because of many fine resources such as those listed in the Appendix. There are tips throughout this book. Also, you'll soon discover that you will accumulate a vast fund of practical knowledge as you work with your students on their projects.

Helping Hand

If you already have experience working with design and technology and feel ready to jump right in, please skip ahead to page 45 where the activities in this book are introduced to you.

Helping Hand

You'll find a set of Planning Sheets in the Appendix, starting on page 130. Use these in any combination to help you prepare.

Helping Hand

Try using a topic web such as the one on page 27 to help you decide on the areas you might need to deal with during your planning.

Time

The good news is that design and technology is not another "add-on" to the time pressures you are already facing as a teacher today. Rather, incorporating design and technology into what you already do will enhance your program and give you more value for your time with students.

The time you allot to any one of the activities in this book is up to you and your students. All of the activities are open-ended, in so far as you can permit students to research the problem, produce their designs and models, evaluate them, then make modifications based on their designs.

In general, allot activities with research components more time, since students will produce much better designs if they have sufficient time to thoroughly research the needs and specifications of the project.

To emphasize problem-solving

This is best done by sticking to a strict time limit at first (use a timer if necessary). Allow students 30 min to discuss and plan their designs. Then, allow 20 min to produce a simple product, such as a drawing, verbal presentation, or model from a construction kit. You should then provide 10 min for evaluation and discussion of the product.

The advantage to this approach is that students learn to focus on the problem-solving aspects of design and technology. You can run through several activities in order to show students how the same strategies can relate to very different situations. We recommend this approach when you are using activities that relate to student experience in some way, so that the lack of prior research will not hinder the generation of testable ideas.

To emphasize evaluation of the product

A key component of the design process is to evaluate or test the product, whether idea, model, or working prototype, against the conditions that were set up as needed to be solved or considered. Even young students quickly grasp the importance of verifying that their designs work! You will find more about this aspect later in the book. We recommend that you allow students the time it takes to improve their designs whether in appearance or function, based on the evaluation result.

Consider these points:

- What is the overall time frame required for the unit?
- Can it be combined with other topics or projects?
- What time frame will be used for activities?
- How often and for how long can the students work on these activities?
- What considerations can you give students who wish to extend the unit?

The Work Area

Where is all this fun going to take place? You should do a bit of preliminary investigation. While your classroom may do just fine, there may be other areas in the school that would be even better for some activities.

General Considerations:

○ You will need a fairly large work area free from clutter, especially if students will be using simple tools. This area should have little traffic. Observe the pathways. Is there enough space for others to get past the workers?

○ Your students will need an area with few distractions. Can you use the hallway or another classroom? If so, will everything have to be moved away each time it is used? This requires additional planning and containers for the materials.

○ Make sure that furniture and equipment is appropriate in size and number for the age range taught. Attempt to have variable working heights suitable for the age group.

○ Try to have separate areas within the work area for a range of practical activities such as construction, wet projects, and graphics.

○ Consider noise levels and adequate lighting when setting up these work areas.

○ If you are working on desks or class tables, consider using art boards or desktop workbenches (bench hooks) to protect tops.

○ If required, arrange for additional storage space.

○ Provide adequate garbage containers, recycling bins, and "junk" boxes for students. Encourage them to place materials in the correct containers at the end of each session.

○ Talk to the principal and custodial staff so that they are aware of the activities you are planning. Your class may at times create remarkable "messes!" Assure them that your students will be responsible for tidying up.

Storage

You'll need space to store materials and tools. Find as much as you can, by sharing with other teachers if necessary. You'll be amazed at how quickly the resources add up once, especially the "found" variety that can take up so much room.

Use shoe boxes for storage of small items and work-in-progress. These slip onto shelves, into desks, and/or into cubbyholes. Deep drawers are good for storing larger unfinished projects. Large plastic tubs with lids are also great. They stack easily and, if you get the clear plastic type, you will be able to see the contents without having to get it off the shelf. Banker's boxes or other large cardboard boxes are good for storing junk material.

Helping Hand

If you can't provide space for work in your classroom, (and don't have access to a workshop), consider working with other teachers to arrange that at least one or two classrooms in your school are made available for design and technology projects.

Helping Hand

An easy way to provide a secure working surface is to use a bench hook, a device that simply fastens on top of a desk or table. You'll find a diagram on how to make a bench hook on page 11.

Helping Hand

Attach a sample item or drawing of the item on the outside of its container to help students find the resources they need – and where to put extras away.

Helping Hand

Try to have real artifacts related to the design topic on display so that students can examine and handle them.

Display Areas

You'll want space to allow students to protect work-in-progress as well as to share their work with others. Can you use hallways, shelves, the office, or the library for exhibits? Consider the need for security of these displays. Make sure that materials and artifacts will not be accidentally knocked over by passing students. Display boxes and cupboards that allow for the display of related two- and three-dimensional items of varying sizes are recommended.

Bulletin board displays should be available to demonstrate different aspects of the design process. Free-standing boards can be used to support this aspect of students' work.

Safety

Helping Hand

A Safety Quiz and Contract for students are provided on pages 147-9 of the Appendix. Use as is, or modify it to suit your school's safety regulations.

- ○ Stress safety with students right from the start. Demonstrate the use of all tools to the students.
- ○ Teach students the appropriate safety measures to be taken while working on design and technology projects.
- ○ Ensure safety equipment is used when required. Make sure students wear safety glasses when using saws and drills.
- ○ Teach students the correct use of all tools before they are allowed to use them.
- ○ Supervise very young children who are working with tools, particularly at the beginning.
- ○ Ensure students know which equipment must be used under adult supervision.

General Points for Students

Go over these points with your students before allowing them to begin any project.

Helping Hand

Safety first. Make sure that you or an adult helper use potentially hazardous equipment such as hot glue guns for very young students.

- ○ If the tool has never been used before, make sure instructions are given on its proper use.
- ○ If unsure, ask the teacher.
- ○ Wear appropriate safety clothing (apron, goggles, strong shoes).
- ○ Make sure long hair or loose clothing is tied back.
- ○ Do not rush about in the workshop area.
- ○ Do not interfere with other people when they are working.
- ○ Tidy tools after use.
- ○ Report any breakages or injuries at once.
- ○ Read labels and instructions carefully.
- ○ Hold or secure the work firmly before cutting or drilling.

Safety Quiz and Contract

Hand these forms out to older students to read then discuss. Go over the main ideas and prepare a safety poster for younger or verbal learners.

What You'll Need

Now that you've thought about where and what your students will be doing, it's time to gather your resources. You will need some basic materials and a few simple tools. You'll develop your classroom inventory as you go along. You should also be thinking about who can help you, both in obtaining resources and in supplying expertise. Perhaps you can enlist the aid and expertise of older students in the school, volunteers, teacher aides, co-op students, parents, etc.

A very important contact to make and nourish is with any technological education specialists in the middle school, junior high or senior school and at the secondary schools in your area. Not only will they be able to supply you with bits and pieces, they will be very interested in your program since this will affect their program in a few years. Invite them to your class to discuss your plans.

Construction Kits

As an introduction to the designing process, construction kits can be used to help the students gain confidence and develop the necessary skills needed for work with other materials. The focus on student-centred learning and the use of these materials is a perfect combination. Very young children need the opportunity to play and experiment with the different materials. The chance to design on their own allows the children the freedom to explore, take chances and try out new ideas. With construction kits, students are given opportunities to:

○ develop an awareness of similarities and differences in size, texture, and colour
○ develop spatial awareness
○ understand the properties of symmetry
○ learn the skills of estimating, experimenting, planning
○ develop an awareness of the importance of design
○ express themselves and extend their language skills through role playing, story telling
○ co-operate and share
○ cope with limitations
○ understand the relationship between cause and effect
○ gain self-confidence.

Children need to be have ample opportunity to explore and create with materials such as construction kits. The use of the construction kits and the design materials will eventually lead the students to the element of control technology where LEGO models can be created that link up to the computer. This interfacing will give the students more opportunities to experiment, explore, and come up with solutions to problems.

Helping Hand

You will find Planning Sheets that deal with the resources you'll need starting on page 130 of the Appendix.

Helping Hand

There is a review of commonly available construction kits, starting on page 137 of the Appendix.

Helping Hand

If necessary, make a schedule or checklist to make sure that all students have an equal opportunity to use the materials.

Strategies For Using Construction Kits

When first introducing construction kits to young children, limit the types and number of pieces to avoid frustration.

It may be necessary to work with small groups of children helping them learn how to fit the pieces together. If some children are reluctant to use the equipment, give them time to explore with one or two other children.

Introduce more items gradually. Teach the children the names of the pieces so that they can identify them correctly. This is important when the more technical kits, such as LEGO Technic, are used with the students.

Managing Costs

One problem that needs to be addressed is the equitable use of these construction kits with all children. When a school is first starting to use these materials, it might be an idea to pool the resources of several classes.

- Start a school library of construction kits. This will help cut down on the initial costs and allow for all children to have an opportunity to use these materials. The more expensive material could be kept in this library.
- Assign student monitors to keep track of the materials.
- Develop a checklist of the items that should be in each kit.
- After each use, check that all of the equipment has been returned. Keep a note of which pieces get mislaid. Track this on an inventory list so you know what has to be replaced.
- Replacement pieces are available for some kits, such as LEGO.
- Ideally, each class should have its own set of LEGO or similar kit as well as sharing the centrally assigned kits.
- Devise a timetable for the construction sets when all of the resources will be available for your class. This should be for a relatively long period of time. Start with 40-50 min a week when the class can work together on building group projects. This amount of time allows the whole class to build together. At the end of the period, all of the objects are dismantled for the next class. Use the hallways for this activity. An unused room in the school could house all of the equipment and kits.
- Store kits in plastic crates for easier storage and movement.
- Try to arrange for parent volunteers to work with groups of children.
- Ensure a cross-curricular approach using theme work. Make use of other resources - the computer, still and video cameras, tape recorder, etc., to provide observational records and feedback on the models.
- Combine the different kits to allow for greater flexibility.
- Use your scrap box to supplement the materials.

Tools

You and your students will be able to produce very successful results with a few simple tools. Such tools can be purchased relatively inexpensively, but make sure that you don't sacrifice quality just to save a few dollars. Consider asking parents to donate any extra tools they may have at home. Work with other teachers in the school to pool resources and share equipment at first until a good-sized collection has been gathered.

Avoid play tools which hold little interest for the children, break easily, and won't do the job properly. They cause frustration, not success. Children are capable of working with real tools, so long as a safe environment exists for their use.

Workbench

A workbench is very useful in a classroom. There are models that can even be folded up and kept out of the way when not in use. The diagram on this page shows a bench hook, a portable workbench that fits over a student desk or table.

Helping Hand

You'll find a wish list of tools suitable for your students on page 136 of the Appendix.

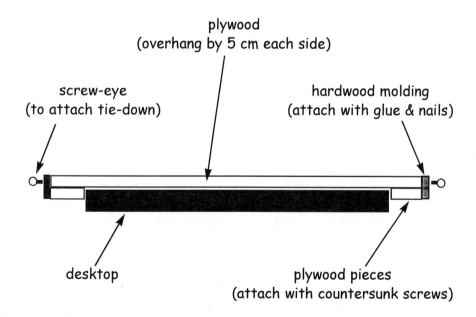

plywood
(overhang by 5 cm each side)

screw-eye
(to attach tie-down)

hardwood molding
(attach with glue & nails)

desktop

plywood pieces
(attach with countersunk screws)

How to make a durable, sturdy bench hook.
(glue a piece of felt to the bottom to protect desktop)

Additional Equipment and Concerns

Safety Glasses

Safety is a very important component of design and technology, just as it is in your usual science teaching. It should be considered at all times in the workshop area. Safety glasses should be available for the children to use, especially when sawing, hammering, or drilling. These are available at hardware, lumber, and automotive supply stores.

Ventilation

Be aware of procedures that should be done only in areas with adequate ventilation. These include: sanding, gluing with liquid glues, spray painting or other finishing that produces fumes, etc.

Information Technology - What tools do your students need to use?

If at all possible, students should also be given opportunities to experiment and become familiar with information technology. Using information technologies effectively will help students extend their intellectual abilities to handle data and information.

Students will benefit from being able to manipulate and present data through the use of the following software tools:

- word processing
- databases
- spreadsheets
- graphics
- Internet exploration software (also called web browsers or search engines) and email software

Helping Hand

You will find a list of useful websites (addresses on the Internet) on page 163 of the Appendix.

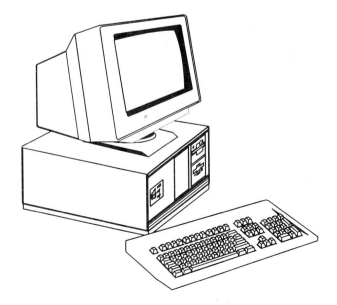

Materials

Students need ample opportunity to experiment with a variety of materials and construction kits so that they will be able to select appropriate materials for their projects.

Let students work with materials for the sake of using them. For instance, allow them opportunities to simply experience hammering pieces of wood and nails. Let them drill holes in wood - don't worry that they are not "making" anything! It is the process, not the product that is being stressed in all technological education activities.

Instruct your students on the proper use of the various materials and tools available to them in the workshop environment.

Working with Wood

Have your students learn to conserve wood by making a model or prototype from a construction kit, paper, or other suitable material before the final project is made from wood.

Sawing Wood

There are many different types of saws that can be used by the students, including a hacksaw, backsaw (tenon saw), and coping saw. Make sure that the wood is securely fastened in the work bench or vise before sawing takes place.

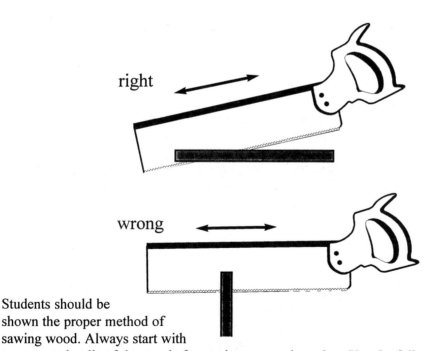

right

wrong

Students should be shown the proper method of sawing wood. Always start with two upward pulls of the saw before trying any push strokes. Use the full length of the saw blade. When the wood is almost cut through, slow down and support the wood to avoid breaking off a splinter and spoiling the cut. Saw the wood in the direction in which it is the thinnest.

Helping Hand

You'll find lists of materials appropriate for your students on pages 31 and 137.

Helping Hand

Encourage the practice of recycling and reusing materials. Parents are a good source of materials, but ask for contributions only when you really need them or risk a storage crisis! Within the school, consider having other teachers, as well as office and custodial staff, set aside useful waste materials for you.

Helping Hand

Pine is one of the easiest woods for students to use because it is soft and easy to saw.

Joining Wood

A simple method of joining wood that yields very good results is to use glue and cardboard corners.

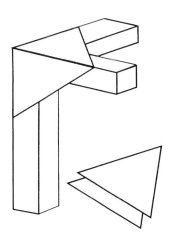

All that is required is bondfast glue, cardboard corners (made from lightweight cardboard), and wood pieces. This method provides a very firm and stable structure.

Shaping Wood

Have students begin using files and rasps are used to shape wood. When shaping wood with these tools, it is important to have the wood held firmly in place with a vise or clamp. The handle of the tool is held in the main hand while the other end is held with the other hand. This makes it easier to control and gives more pressure. All files and rasps are used on the push stroke. Once shaped, the wood will be ready to be finished with sandpaper.

Drilling Wood

Students sometimes need to make holes in their projects. Hand drills can be used quite successfully even with younger children. Students can use power drills once proper instructions have been given and safety discussed. Before drilling, work must be held in place with a clamp or a vise. Put a piece of wood behind or under the work to be drilled to protect the work from splintering when the drill comes through. Protect the surface where drilling takes place - the bench hook, table, or work bench - with a scrap of wood.

Using a Chisel

Chisels can also be used to shape wood. There are a variety of types of chisels that give different effects. Wood chiselled in the direction of the grain splits easily. A split, once started, usually goes farther than needed. Because the chisel follows the grain, it doesn't always go in the right direction. A saw cut at the end of the desired length ensures that only the correct amount of wood is removed. The wood being chiselled must be firmly clamped or in a vise. Keep both hands behind the cutting edge and always cut away from your body. Make a saw cut first and try to chisel across the grain. Use a wooden mallet if there is a need to strike the handle of the chisel.

Working with Electricity

If your students will be building circuits and using electricity in their designs, you will need the following supplies in your classroom:

Batteries

Small batteries are usually 1.5 V each. One of the most common battery is the C cell which is 1.5 V. Dry cell batteries are 4.5 V.

Wire

There are several types of wire suitable for this purpose.

○ Flex is wire covered with plastic. The single strand variety is the easiest to use. The wire needs to be stripped before it can be used. About 3 cm of the plastic needs to be removed from the wire. Use wire strippers for this. Be careful to remove only the plastic without cutting through the wire. Two strand flex wire needs to be separated before it is used.

○ Florist's wire is a thin, flexible wire without any covering on it.

○ Glazed copper wire is a shiny copper wire coated with varnish. It is used to make electromagnets.

Lights, Bulbs

Small lights with screw-in bulbs can be used safely. The voltage rating of the bulb should match or exceed that of the battery. For example, use a 2.5 volt bulb with a 1.5 volt battery.

Bulb Holders

Bulb holders allow students to connect bulbs more easily to the battery.

Battery Holders

Commercial battery holders are the easiest. These can be purchased at electrical supply stores or hobby shops. The holders will take 1, 2 or 4 batteries and come in sizes for different types of batteries.

Motors

Small hobby motors can be used as an energy source. These motors can be obtained through hobby shops and electrical supply stores. The most common type is the 1.5 volt motor. The motor in the LEGO DACTA (R) kits is 4.5 volt.

Switches

A switch is just a break in a circuit and students often create their own switching mechanism from everyday materials as part of their design. Commercially available switches can be purchased at hobby shops and electrical supply stores.

Helping Hand

Each used Polaroid film pack contains a 6 V battery with much of its charge still remaining. Students can connect wires easily to these batteries. (Connect the wires to both exposed areas of foil to complete the circuit.) This is an inexpensive method to obtain power for testing prototypes.

Helping Hand

Avoid using old donated electrical components in student constructions for safety reasons. However, students can learn a great deal from dismantling electrical devices such as toasters. Just remove the power cord before allowing students to explore.

Do's and Don'ts When Using Circuits

DO

○ Stress safety always!

○ If you are not familiar with the topic, make lots of circuits yourself before you work with students. Use equipment that fits together easily and works the way it is supposed to.

○ Match the battery voltage and the bulb voltage. The voltage of the bulb should match or exceed that of the battery.

○ Standardize your equipment so that you only have one type of battery or battery holder at first.

○ Make sure that students understand that each battery has two contact points and each device (bulb, buzzer, motor, etc.) has two connecting points. These have to be joined together to complete a circuit or circle to make it work.

○ Start by connecting various devices one by one to the batteries to make a series of complete circuits. Introduce the switch as a controlling device.

DON'T

○ Set puzzle circuits that are difficult to explain.

○ Move too quickly to explanations if students have not had much background experience.

○ Start with electrostatics and expect students to see the connection with current electricity.

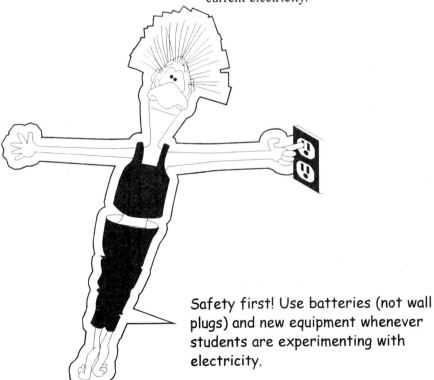

Safety first! Use batteries (not wall plugs) and new equipment whenever students are experimenting with electricity.

Community, Parent Involvement

Let parents know of your plans. They are often able to provide materials, tools, and time to help you. Send home a letter explaining the goals of your design and technology program.

Ask for volunteers from the community. Many older adults are willing to lend a hand.

Send a letter to local industries and tell them of your design and technology program. Ask for their help. They will want to encourage this type of activity and they may have lots of materials to donate. Arrange to pick up the materials and make a personal connection.

Tips for your helpers

○ Share with your adult and/or student helpers the aims of your program.

○ Remind them not to do all the work. They should be careful not to interfere with a child's plan.

○ They should offer encouragement. Children need to be encouraged at this early age to be creative and inventive. For example, if a four-year old wants to try something, encourage the child to try it, while being available to assist as needed.

○ They should allow discovery. Let students discover on their own, for example, that a car with wheels glued on will not move. Provide opportunities for them to discover these concepts on their own and to try different solutions to the problem.

○ They should use appropriate language with students - talk to them in a thoughtful, serious, respectful manner and use language students understand.

○ Students should feel that others value their opinions and views, and that you will not do their thinking or talking for them.

Helping Hand

You will find a planning sheet with space to record community contacts in the Appendix on page 133.

Helping Hand

An adult may do some of the initial work for younger children. As children gain experience and confidence, they can do more of the sawing and hammering. And older helpers should handle any potentially hazardous procedures for young children, such as using hot glue guns.

Dealing with "What do I do now?"

This will likely be the most commonly heard question from your students at first. Try to eliminate the "what do I do now?" attitude at an early age. It is important to foster a questioning attitude but it is also important to develop an independent, creative, and confident approach to solving problems.

○ When students ask, "What do I do now?," ask for their suggestions for solving the problem.

○ Ask other class members as well. See if anyone else has a suggestion.

The time you spend developing in students a questioning attitude, and in developing their independence is very important. Your students will progress naturally if they have opportunities to work with materials and are praised for their efforts.

Remember:

Students should make their own decisions.

Praise is essential.

Don't give your answer -- it's only one possible solution after all.

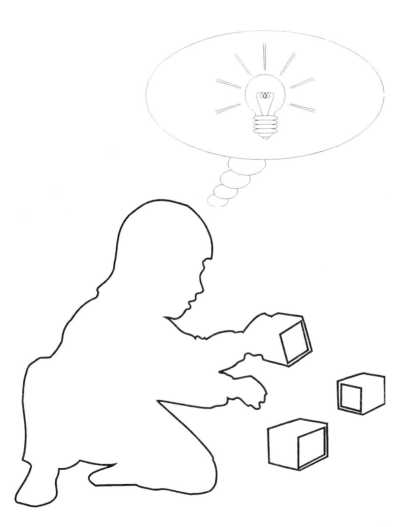

CONTENT AND CURRICULUM

Since every jurisdiction differs slightly from others in curriculum emphasis and terminology, please add, change, or substitute what is used in the following discussion as appropriate for your own needs. Listed outcomes are based on the minimum general outcomes that are achieved through the design and technology approach in this book. We are certain you will find many more that are accommodated as well.

Progression of Technological Concepts and Skills: From Play to Process

We highly recommend that all schools begin to expose children to the design and technology process as early as possible. These programs are interdisciplinary in nature and deal with technology as it is found in any subject matter in every learning area. As they proceed from kindergarten to grade 6, children should explore the variety of technological processes and products that are already present in their programs. Correct terminology should be used, particularly as it relates to the central concepts (structures, materials, fabrication, mechanisms, power and energy, control and systems, function, aesthetics and ergonomics). Students should begin to recognize these concepts as they encounter them in all school subjects and outside the classroom, at home, in the community or in the natural environment.

We suggest that the initial explorations of technology begin in a playful manner. Then, as students progress through grades 4-6, they will use a design process and inquiry techniques to plan the processes and construct the products. The complexity of the activities depends on the ability and interests of the child. All students should develop skills in solving technological problems both by themselves and in small groups.

A Progression of Materials and How to Use Them

There is a natural progression in the use of different materials and associated skills. A suggested progression is:

○ soft materials - water, sand, clay, Plasticine
○ hard/soft materials - paper, cardboard, fabric
○ hard materials - plastic, wood, everyday materials, construction kits
○ desire for movement - simple wheels, pivots, hinges, pulleys
○ motorizing - rubber bands, wind, water, electric motors
○ action - lights, bells, pumps
○ control - progress through manual, electrical, and computer control.

Give children ample time to explore and experiment with different materials. This provides them with the background knowledge needed to select the appropriate material for different activities. Skills are acquired through continued application in as wide a variety of circumstances as possible. Encourage children to try new ideas and use different materials as new problems are encountered.

A Progression through Product

Children need opportunities to experiment and explore on their own before guided or directed activities are introduced. Young children should be encouraged to make models, draw pictures of the model, and then write about their designs. In this way, young children are moving from the concrete to the abstract. As students mature, they can be encouraged to design and sketch their models and then construct them. Modifications can be made to the models as required. Children should have a sound understanding of simple structures and mechanisms before any type of movement and power takes place.

A Progression of Lessons and Activities

It is important when students are working on design and technology activities to follow a sequential progression of lessons and activities. This ensures that students achieve the following set of outcomes.

The Outcomes

By the end of the elementary grades, students should be able to show that they:

○ realize that there are numerous solutions to any given problem.
○ recognize opportunities for problem-solving activities.
○ can identify the problem situation.
○ can generate a variety of ideas and possible solutions.
○ are able to work within a variety of themes and contexts for developing design proposals.
○ can develop the best solutions and ideas using appropriate resources.
○ can create working diagrams and models throughout the design process.
○ can construct a prototype of the model.
○ can test the solution using a variety of criteria.
○ can modify the solution, if necessary.
○ can use information technology appropriately and effectively to communicate and handle information in a variety of forms and for a variety of purposes.
○ can record the results of the procedures.
○ can evaluate their own work and the work of others in terms of technological components and effects of the design.
○ can work on design problems individually and in groups.
○ consider safety factors in all areas.
○ understand the role of technology in the context of self, school, family, community, and the environment.

Cross-curricular Outcomes

The nature of design and technology, to engage in problem-solving in the context of a situation, lends itself well to cross-curricular outcomes such as those listed below.

Links in Math, Science, and Technology

Science

Students should show:

- an understanding of the natural world
- they can use the investigative approach
- skill in direct experience, logical analysis, clarification of ideas through discussion, and comparison
- they can devise experiments and tests
- they can design solutions to problems
- an ability to blend science and technology
- an ability to use elements of science in design activities
- they can manipulate scientific equipment such as balances, levers, and other mechanisms

Math

Students should show:

- that they understand and experience a variety of models, structures, patterns, symmetries
- the ability to use measurement, estimation, calculation, comparison
- the ability to enhance communication skills through visual presentation
- they can explore relationships of size, shape, classification
- they can reflect upon appropriate strategies for completing purposeful activities.

Technology

Students should show:

- the ability to make informed choices about their environment
- an appreciation of the natural and manufactured world
- the ability to respond to their environment
- an understanding of form and structure using a variety of materials
- the ability to use correct technical terminology
- the ability to use trial and experiment in order to make objects that work
- appropriate group work habits
- problem-solving at a simple level
- an understanding of the need for safe work habits.

Links with Outcomes of Other Curriculum Areas

Communication (Language Arts)

Students should show:

○ the ability to engage in much dialogue while involved in these activities
○ the ability to form clear statements of what has to be done
○ the use of questions to get further information
○ the use language for a purpose
○ the generation of a technical vocabulary
○ the development of a variety of modes of expression
○ the refinement of skills of accuracy, clarity, brevity, and sequencing in writing and speaking
○ they have acquired technical writing skills
○ the development of editing and presenting skills
○ the ability to reflect critically on work
○ they appreciate an exchange of viewpoints
○ they can listen and respond sensitively to others
○ the development of feelings of trust.

Self & Society (Social Studies, Geography, History)

Students should show:

○ an understanding of the relationship between people and the environment
○ a recognition that the world is in a constant process of change
○ an appreciation of cultural diversity
○ an ability to analyze home, school, and other environments through observation, maps, drawings, models
○ an understanding of how natural resources (and lack of them) have influenced our environmental development
○ the ability to create designs that make the environment safer, cleaner
○ they can identify the common technology in use today.

Physical Education

Students should show:

○ the development of an understanding of the mechanisms of the human body
○ they have become aware of equipment that extends human capabilities
○ an appreciation of the use of technology in sport, e.g., the curve in a hockey stick, stringing tennis racquets.

Visual Arts

Students should show:

- they can investigate objects
- they can represent objects from observation and imagination
- the ability to model and communicate ideas about how objects could work as an aid to understanding how objects do work
- the ability to draw, model
- an understanding of colour, shape, size, form, texture, signs, symbols
- they can transform material
- they can create objects of aesthetic value
- they can make critical judgements.

Music

Students should show:

- they have explored the characteristics and properties of sound and music as a universal language
- they can construct musical instruments
- the ability to create computer generated music.

Drama

Students should show:

- the development of self awareness and self confidence
- they can re-enact stories using a technological approach
- they can retell stories.

Other Outcomes

Among the benefits of design and technology when performed in an atmosphere that is cross-curricular, rather than focussing on design and technology as a subject, are the following more widely applicable outcomes that can be achieved.

Technology

Students should show:

○ they can consider "how will it be made?" and "how will it work?"

○ an understanding of how natural and physical resources can be and have been used to solve problems arising from human needs

○ the acquisition of model-building, construction, and communication skills

○ they can apply scientific concepts

○ they can get out and put away resources

○ they can use tools in a purposeful way and organize classroom space

○ they can move around the school

Using Tools

Students should be given opportunities to develop skills and a level of co-ordination and control in the safe use of:

○ hand tools

○ machinery and equipment - work benches, safety glasses, etc.

○ cameras (Polaroid, 35 mm film or digital, video)

○ computers and appropriate peripherals.

Students should demonstrate the ability to perform the the following operations:

○ cutting

○ drilling

○ forming/shaping

○ joining

○ folding

○ using adhesives

Communication

Students should be given opportunities to:

○ use appropriate vocabulary

○ ask relevant questions

○ present information both verbally and in written form

○ construct graphs to show information

○ manipulate data - databases, spreadsheets, graphs.

Working with Others

Students should be given opportunities to:

- contribute to the team
- listen to the ideas of others
- value the skills of others
- ask for and accepting other people's preferences
- accept the opinions of others
- take responsibility for being a member of a team
- work with others and helping when necessary.

Organization and Planning

Students should be given opportunities to:

- identify what needs to be done
- plan ways in which tasks can be completed
- change plans when necessary
- use time and resources wisely
- appreciate constraints and working within them
- persevere
- reflect on how projects could be modified for improvement.

Evaluation

Students should be given opportunities to:

- evaluate individual work using a specific set of criteria
- evaluate the work of others using established criteria
- evaluate their individual effectiveness within a group.

Helping Hand

Forms for self, peer, and group evaluation are provided on pages 152-7 in the Appendix.

An Example of Cross-curricular Links

This web illustrates some of the opportunities to link different curriculum areas under just one area of technology, in this case transportation. You could use a similar approach to visualize your own cross-curricular planning around a technological concept.

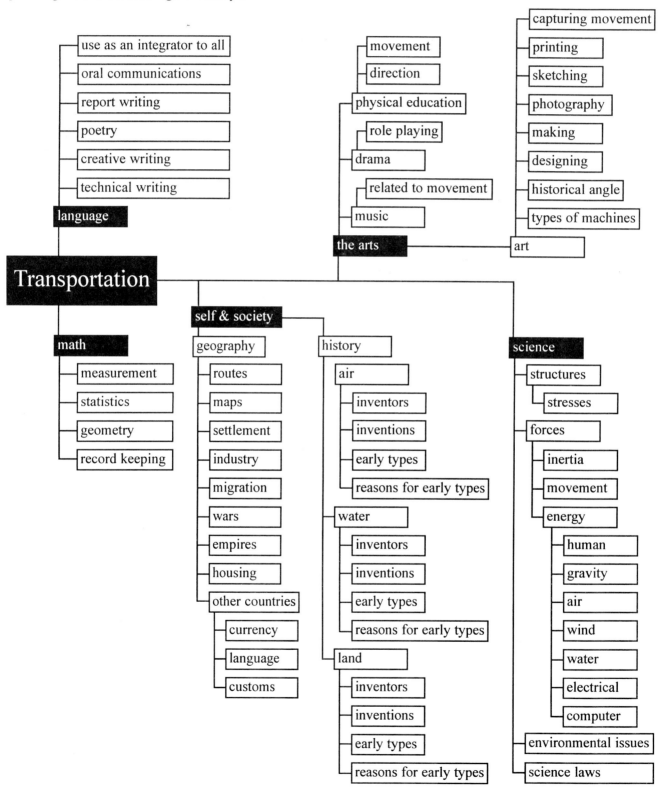

An Example of a Planning Web

Use this web as a quick reminder of the planning areas you may wish to consider when incorporating design and technology into your program.

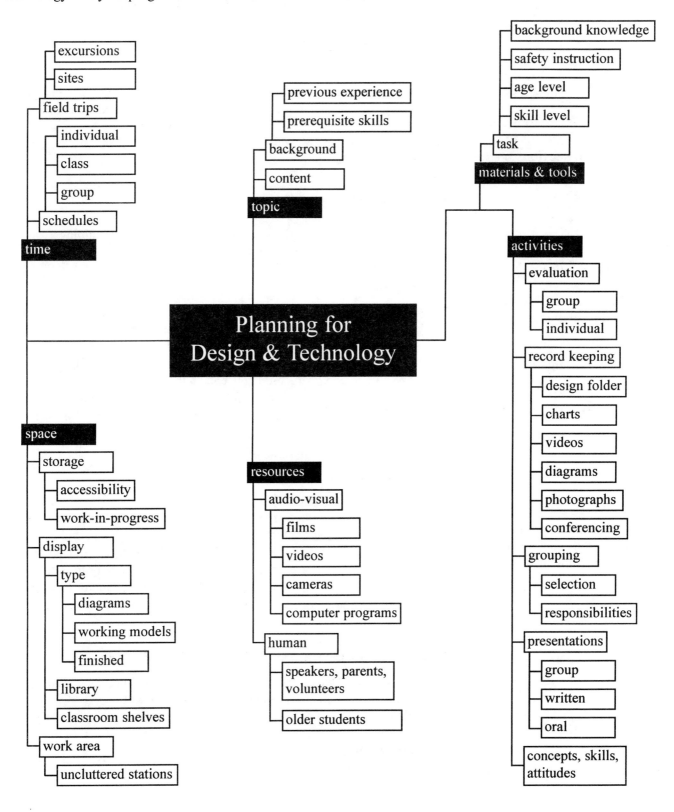

A GUIDE TO INTRODUCING BASIC CONCEPTS IN DESIGN AND TECHNOLOGY

Basic Concepts

There are ten central concepts, grouped into three major sections, in this book.

> Fabrication
>> structures
>> materials
>> mechanisms
>
> Motion
>> power and energy
>> control and systems
>
> Human Elements
>> function
>> aesthetics
>> ergonomics

The forces acting on a structure are either **static** (not moving) or **dynamic** (moving). Static forces are not as destructive as dynamic forces.

This section lists ideas and terminology that you may find useful when you are introducing design and technology activities to your class. Background information for you is provided first, followed by recommendations on appropriate terms and procedures for grades K-3 and 4-6. Modify these lists to best suit your program.

Fabrication

Fabrication deals with the act or process of forming and assembling structures, mechanisms, and materials.

Structures

A structure is any supporting framework, such as the skeleton that supports a person's body. In design and technology, structures are the essential physical or conceptual parts of an object. Students need to appreciate the ways in which various structures are constructed or organized. Students should be able to apply structural concepts to the design of load-bearing structures. This will allow them to build stronger and more stable walls, objects, bridges, etc. Structures usually have one or more of the following uses:

- to support a load (water tower)
- to span a gap (bridge)
- to enclose objects or people (car).

A structure's strength is more important than its appearance and cost. If a structure cannot resist the forces that act on it, it will collapse and be worthless. Both external and internal forces act upon a structure. The forces in a structure result in the structure being acted upon by one or more of the following: tension and/or compression, bending, shearing, and/or torsion. To keep the form of an object, the internal forces must match the external forces.

Making Stronger and/or More Flexible Structures

By changing the shape of materials, the structure can gain (or lose) strength or flexibility. These changes can be created by the use of:

folding	cellular forms
girders	triangulation
corrugation	

Folding

Most thin materials are flexible. Folding a sheet of cardboard in half lengthwise doubles the thickness, but it will still be flexible and will not have increased its rigidity very much. Opening up that sheet of card lengthwise so that each half is at right angles to the other makes the card more rigid. A card shaped in this fashion is a simple L-shaped girder.

Girders

Girders can be made more complex and therefore sturdier by using more folds. Box girders form an enclosed space. A box girder with 4 sides is less rigid than a triangular girder with 3 sides. A tube (like a bicycle frame) is a kind of a box girder.

Corrugation

Corrugation involves repeated or concertina folding of materials. Folds made across the paper or card makes the card more flexible than card with corrugations running lengthwise. The increased rigidity is only in the direction at right angles to the folds. If a corrugated sheet is glued between two sheets of paper, some of its flexibility is reduced and the sandwich produced is more rigid in all directions. It is still most rigid at right angles to the direction of the folds An example is corrugated paper.

Cellular Forms

Combining several tubes made from card or paper into cellular forms produces a structure that is effective at resisting pressure applied to the ends of the tubes, i.e. **compression**. These shapes are used where strength and lightness are both very important such as the floor panels of an airplane. Cellular structures can also save money because a cheap material can be used in place of a more expensive one.

Triangulation

The triangle is a strong **rigid** shape and is used a great deal in structural work. For example, a triangular form made from three pieces of wood or card, is strong and secure. Shapes lacking **triangulation** are not as rigid.

If you add another strip (strut made from card) diagonally from one corner to another in a square shape, it becomes more rigid. (The rectangle has been divided into two triangles.) If a second strip was added between the other two corners, the shape would not become any stronger.

If a **tie** (string) is used instead of a **strut** (card) the rectangle becomes stronger in one direction but not the other. By adding a second tie as a diagonal, the rectangle now becomes totally rigid again. Ties are much lighter than struts so if weight is important, ties can be an alternative to struts even though two are needed. The problem with ties is finding the correct tension.

Helping Hand

You will find an illustrated glossary starting on page 156 of the Appendix.

Helping Hand

Combine hands-on work with triangulation into your mathematics lessons on geometric shapes.

Helping Hand

If your students are investigating bridges, have them look up these types: arch, beam, truss, cantilever, suspension, and moving bridges. Take a field trip to examine local bridges, or show students slides or videotapes.

Structures in K-3

Young students should be exposed to terms such as weak, strong, heavy, support, and force. The use of manipulative materials such as construction kits, containers, boxes, empty plastic bottles, etc. should be used to help children understand some of the basic elements of structures. They can experiment with building and knocking down walls made from a variety of materials. Get the children experimenting with weight-bearing principles by putting books or simple weights on top of their structures to see the effects.

Experiment with the strength of different shapes by using simple materials like popsicle sticks and strips of construction paper. Have the children discover about the strength of triangles through these guided activities. Direct the activities to allow the children to discover different methods of making objects stronger. Folding paper in a variety of methods can be introduced.

Co-ordinate these activities with your math program. Use different shapes such as cylinders and cubes for these activities. Have the children discover which of these shapes provides the greatest support to a structure.

Important Terms To Understand

strong/weak	mass
heavy/light	weight
long/short	force
support	

Important Concepts to Understand

struts and ties
folding
corrugation
use of triangles and simple 2-D geometry

Students should demonstrate that they can: create structural designs that will support a mass.

Structures in 4-6

Important Terms to Understand

strong/weak	mass
heavy/light	weight
long/short	force
support	

Important Concepts to Understand

tension/compression
shearing/torsion
cellular forms
the use of simple 3-D geometry.

Students should demonstrate that they can: create more complex structural designs that will support a mass.

MATERIALS

Materials are the basic substances or information from which a structure is made. It is important that students use a variety of materials when working in design and technology. There is a natural progression of the materials used by them.

The use of appropriate materials is linked to other technological concepts and must be considered along with each particular area. Children should be exposed to a wide variety of materials.

A Guide to Appropriate Materials When Planning Design Activities

Students should explore the physical and aesthetic properties of the following natural and manufactured materials:

water	plasticine
sand	clay
paper	plastics
cardboard	wood
fabric	bonding substances

Students should be familiar with the following properties:

hard/soft	elastic/inelastic
brittle/flexible	rough/smooth (texture)
pliable/rigid	shiny/dull (finish)

The properties of the material will determine which tools are used.

Materials in K-3

Students should be able to use the following materials appropriately:

simple construction kits (to make models)
everyday junk materials (cardboard tubes, egg cartons)
plastic materials (straws, tubing, plastic bags, plastic wrap).

Students should be able to select and use the following tools correctly and safely:

bench hook or mitre box	junior hacksaw
hammer	ruler
hand drill	scissors
hole punch	screwdriver

Students should be aware of the following factors related to materials:

weight	availability
cost	decomposition (recyclable)

Helping Hand

When working on models, encourage students to use materials that have properties similar to that of the real thing, e.g., concrete could be represented by plaster of Paris or clay.

Materials in 4-6

Students should explore the physical and aesthetic properties of the following natural and manufactured materials:

wood
plaster
clay
metal

Students should be able to select and use the following tools correctly and safely:

awl	mitre box
chisel	plane
compass	pliers
drill bits	sanding tools
drill press (table variety)	spring clamp
files	T-square
glue guns	vise
wire cutters	wire strippers
junior cutting knife	

Students should be able to manipulate and use the following factors as they relate to the production of the design project:

weight
cost
availability
decomposition (recyclable)

MECHANISMS

Mechanisms are the parts of a structure that allow it to work or function. When students understand the basic principles related to structures, they can begin to include mechanisms in their designs. If the basic concepts related to structures are not fully understood by students, they will experience difficulty working with mechanisms and will not have the necessary knowledge required to modify their designs.

Types of Mechanisms

All machines are made up of one or more **mechanisms** used to solve a particular problem. They can only work when **energy** is applied. All types of mechanisms can be divided into simple machines -- levers, pulleys, wheels/axles, inclined plane -- that have been developed over time to form the basis of more complex machines

Basic Concepts

- A mechanism can be used to turn one kind of force into another kind of force.
- Mechanisms can only produce work when energy is supplied.
- All mechanisms make work easier.
- Mechanisms use or create motion.
- A mechanism may increase the speed of an operation or increase the distance travelled.
- A mechanism may increase the force that operates.
- Several mechanisms can be combined to form a machine.
- Mechanisms are used because they are very versatile and efficient.

Basic Vocabulary

All simple machines involve certain principles. The following terms are typically used when discussing how well simple machines perform their tasks. Depending on your students, try to use as many of these terms as possible.

> force
> distance
> work
> load
> effort
> energy
> friction
> mechanical advantage
> velocity ratio

Helping Hand

Please refer to the Glossary on page 158 for definitions of terms.

Making Mechanisms from Ordinary Materials

Making Pulleys

Pulleys are easily obtainable, but students can make their own as follows.

- ○ Find or cut three round discs from heavy cardboard or wood.
- ○ Make one disc smaller than the other two.
- ○ Find the exact center of each disc and drill a small hole in each.
- ○ Glue the three discs together, the outside discs being the larger ones.
- ○ In order for the pulley to run smoothly, the axle bearings must be smooth (the bearings are the holes in which axles rotate).
- ○ Use a piece of dowel for the axle (rod).
- ○ Attach each end of the axle to a stationary object.
- ○ Wrap a string around the container twice to use as a pulling device.

If you see students having problems, check these characteristics:

- ○ The pulleys must be in line with each other.
- ○ The axles must be parallel.
- ○ The belt must be correctly tensioned.

Making a More Effective Pulley

To increase the force of a pulley, there must be a greater distance from the object. For example, to move a load two metres, the distance away from the pulley must be four metres. The distance is always two times effort. With two ropes, force is exerted over twice the distance the load moves, and the pulley lifts with twice the force.

Helping Hand

Pulleys can also be made from objects such as plastic film containers. Make a hole through each end and push a skewer or piece of dowel through for the axle.

Simple Machines

lever

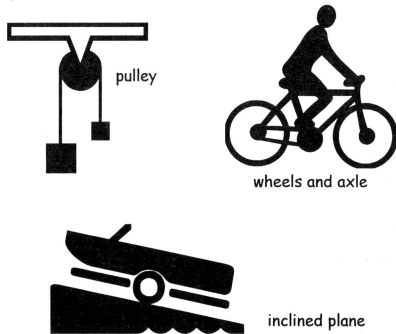

pulley

wheels and axle

inclined plane

Making Axle Bearings and Wheels

A variety of materials can be used to make axle bearings and wheels. Encourage students to be creative in their use of junk material.

- ❍ All axle bearings must be long enough to enable the wheels, bearings, washers, and end stoppers to be fitted easily. It is better to trim off the surplus axle when the vehicle is complete than to cram everything on a short axle and find that the wheels don't turn. It doesn't really matter if a little extra axle is sticking out the end past the end stoppers.
- ❍ To keep the wheels in place, end stoppers can be made from materials such as Plasticine or glue.

Making More Effective Levers

There are several ways to increase the effect of a lever.

- ❍ Increasing the distance between the effort and the fulcrum increases the load that can be moved.
- ❍ Moving the fulcrum to one end decreases the length of the load arm.
- ❍ Shortening the load arm reduces the force (effort) required; the lever lifts more.
- ❍ Moving the fulcrum even closer to the load means that the effort arms must move a greater distance. As the effort moves closer to the fulcrum, more force is applied. The longer the lever, the greater its mechanical advantage is. For example, in a row boat, a person's arms move a small distance in order to get a larger movement at the other end. This in turn gives speed. Both ends of the oar (lever) move at the same speed but the longer end (the load arm) moves a greater distance in the same time.

Other Mechanisms

Gears

Before students start to work with more complex mechanisms, introduce them to the concept of gears and how gears can be used to change speed and direction of objects. **Gears** are forms of wheels and axles. One toothed wheel turns another toothed wheel and interlocks with it. Gears are often used to co-ordinate parts that travel at different speeds, for example, in watch mechanisms.

The Inclined Plane

The inclined plane is another simple machine that makes work easier. An inclined plane is not as obvious to students as other machines. A slope, such as the side of the hill, is a natural inclined plane. A ramp is an inclined plane made by people. Other examples are the cutting edge of knives, the threads on screws, and ramps that use an inclined plane to help move an object even though the ramp does not move. Less force is needed to move something up a hill, because the plane bears some of the load. The flatter the incline, the greater the distance the object must move and the more force the plane applies. An inclined plane can be made more compact. This is

Helping Hand

You will find an illustrated glossary starting on page 156 of the Appendix.

Students can use pulleys to move objects with less force. Pulleys can also be used to change the direction of movement. And they can be used to change speed. If a large pulley is connected by a belt to a small pulley, the small pulley turns faster. So if a large pulley drives a small one, there is an increase in speed. If a small pulley drives a large one, there is a decrease in speed.

---

seen in roads that bend and twist, as well as stairs around a stadium.

Screws, another form of inclined plane, hold things together better than nails. The threads, or spirals, of screws have a much stronger grip than nails. This is why almost all complex machines are put together with screws. Screws are not only threaded but tapered. They act as a wedge as well as an inclined plane. A nail is a wedge only, so a greater force is needed to drive in a nail. In a screw, less force is required because it is applied over a greater distance.

Mechanisms in K-3

Students should be able to use the following mechanisms:

> levers
> pulleys
> wheels and axles (includes gears)
> inclined plane (includes the wedge and screw).

Students should be familiar with the following concepts:

> changing direction and speed
> overcoming inertia
> slippage

Mechanisms in Grades 4-6

Students should be able to use the following mechanisms:

> linkages   cranks
> gears   sprocket and chains
> ratchet and pawl   block and tackle
> rack and pinion   cams

Students should be familiar with the following concepts:

> mechanical advantage
> gear ratio
> increasing and reducing movement

MOTION

Motion deals with the various forms of movement. The topics related to motion are covered under the two major topics of power and energy, and control and systems. Include in your studies as many different forms of movement as you and your students can imagine.

Power and Energy

Once students have had ample experience in structures, materials, and mechanisms, they can progress to creating models that employ different types of power or energy.

A typical progression from beginner to more experienced student would be:

human   gravity   air   elastic   spring   water   electric
——▶

Basic Concepts

○ Moving things have energy (as do non-moving things, of course, though stored until released).

○ Movement is caused by things pushing or pulling one another. When this happens, work is done. **Work** is the key word here. It involves both the push or pull (the energy) and the movement caused by it. The pull may be from gravity, a force, in which case the energy causes movement downwards.

○ Doing physical work uses energy.

○ Machines and animals use energy in order to move. People and animals obtain energy from food. Machines use the energy contained in fuel, oil (hydraulics), moving air (wind and pneumatics), and other substances.

○ Energy can be stored.

○ Stored or potential energy can be released in a number of ways. Water can be poured from a height so that it sets free kinetic energy in falling. Burning oil or gas produces energy in the form of heat. Stretched elastic bands and wound up clock mechanisms contain stored energy, which becomes active when the springs or bands are released to make things move (kinetic energy.)

○ Heat can do work.

○ A great deal of kinetic energy comes from heat. When something is hotter than its surroundings, a push (force) may be created which can make something move. Car engines, hot air balloons, and rockets take advantage of the heat released during chemical reactions and change this into kinetic energy (the movement of mechanisms).

Helping Hand

In design and technology, the terms power and energy have historically been used to refer to any resources that enable a mechanism to perform work. Teachers more familiar with scientific usage of these terms may find the use here to be different in some respects. You should aim for consistency within your treatment as far as possible.

Work = force x distance, therefore, in a technological sense, work only takes place if motion occurs.

Most energy comes from the sun. Plants produce food using sunlight. In turn, animals store energy by eating plants. Oil, coal, and wood are or were all plant products. Air moves because of high and low pressure areas caused by heat from the sun.

Using Human Power

There are several forces that students can apply to cause movement. These include:

> lifting;
> pulling;
> pushing;
> twisting (winding handles, turning keys);
> blowing (musical instruments, balloons), etc.

Using Gravity

This energy is seen in two modes:

> free fall (a falling weight can trigger an event, such as an alarm);
> controlled drop (slides, pendulums).

Using Air Power

Air can be used as a source of power in several ways.

> windmills (used to pump water, turn fair rides, grind corn);
> wind powered vehicles (cars, boats, yachts, kites);
> jet propulsion (rockets, cars, balloons, boats);
> pneumatic effects (to raise and lower machines);
> resistance (parachutes, escape mechanisms).

Using Elastic Bands

Elastic bands can be used in three different ways:

- ○ Twisted Elastic - If an elastic band is twisted tightly and then released, the object to which it is attached will shoot out at a high speed.

- ○ Stretched Elastic - If an elastic band is connected between two axles and then turned round and round in one direction. it will wind itself onto the axle and become stretched longer and longer. When the axle is released, it will rotate rapidly in the opposite direction to which it was wound. The axle will continue to spin under its own momentum.

- ○ Compressed Elastic - This is seen in the elastic material compressed inside golf and other sports balls.

Helping Hand

Some students may be confused that elastic bands make energy. Be sure they understand that the elastic simply releases stored energy put into it prior to use.

Using Springs

There are three main types of springs.

○ compression (used for firing objects such as the ball in a pinball machine);

○ extension (used for hanging objects such as ceiling lights which can be raised and lowered);

○ torsion (twisting) (used in hinges of lids that "spring open")

Using Water Power

Students can use water power in many ways. Just be sure you have a work area that can easily be cleaned and is safe to have wet.

hydraulic power (syringes and tubing);

harnessing the power of flowing water (water wheel).

Using Electricity

There is more information about using electricity in your classroom on page 15. Basically, students can use electricity to power one of the following devices:

lights (bulbs, LED's);

movement (motors);

sound (buzzers);

heat (hot wire tools);

magnetism (electromagnetic devices).

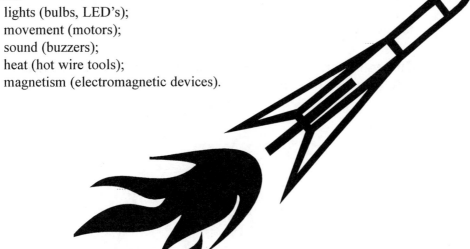

Helping Hand

Make sure that all students are thinking about safety when they work with or near heat sources. Younger students may need to be reminded that heat can cause burns.

Motion for K-3

Students should be able to use the following sources of energy safely and appropriately:

human
gravity
air
elastic
spring
water
electric

Students should be aware of the following energy sources and their hazards:

steam (burns)
chemical (burns)
heat (burns and fire)
sound (hearing loss)

Motion for 4-6

Students should be able to use the following sources of energy safely and appropriately:

pneumatic
hydraulic
solar
electromagnetic
electronic

Students should be aware of the effects of the following energy sources and their hazards:

steam (burns)

chemical (burns)

heat (burns and fire)

sound (hearing loss)

radioactive (understand the concepts)

CONTROL AND SYSTEMS

Control is the means by which a mechanism is regulated. Systems are comprehensive, self-sustaining combinations of interrelated structures, mechanisms, etc., which may be connected to other systems.

Example of a control - a simple switch that only turns lights on and off

Example of a system - a simple switch connected to a computer programmed to use the switch to turn the lights on and off in a prescribed sequence.

Examples of simple controls:

strings - marionettes;

lever - puppets;

electrical switches - lights;

pneumatics - balloons;

hydraulics - syringes.

Progression of Lessons

After students have had experience with construction kits and simple design materials, there will be an interest in applying methods of control to the objects. We have found that students need to have the prerequisite background knowledge and skills in the areas of structures, materials, mechanisms, and power and energy before control activities are introduced.

Students can start with elementary manual control systems to check if things are working. Simple switches and interfaces can be used initially. The next step is the use of handheld control systems such as the LEGO DACTA (R) materials. The final step is the use of the computer to control the movement of objects.

Note: If you don't have access to computers or commercial kits, your students can still do great designs and models using conventional, easily available materials.

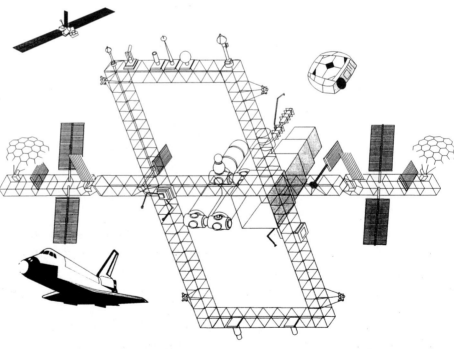

Basic Concepts

O Control involves making things work as expected, such as moving the limbs on a card figure, steering a model boat, or using microwave ovens to cook.

O Control is used in conjunction with forms of energy, such as switches and motors with electricity.

O Control is used in many everyday objects to make our lives easier and more comfortable, including cars, telephones, home heating, and televisions.

O Control often involves the use of computers to program a set of instructions, such as seen in programmable toys, banking machines, or computer games.

Helping Hand

You will find more information on electricity and switches on page 15.

Types of Control

A wide variety of devices can be used to control the operation of objects. Control can be seen as: "Making things do what we want them to do." There are many different methods of controlling objects in everyday life. Students can use different means to "control" (cause) the operation of something. Many toys designed to stimulate young children use methods of control, e.g., push a button and a bell rings.

Computer Control

An **interface** is any device that allows various input and output devices to be safely linked to the computer keyboard. Having an interface turns a computer into a switch that can control a number of objects, switching them on and off (**outputs**.) There is usually some means by which the computer responds to incoming information from various sensors (**inputs**). Typical inputs from sensors can detect changes in movement, pressure, light, and heat conditions through: rocker switches, reed switches, pressure pads, tilt switches (mercury), and/or photoelectric cells

Once the input has been received, the computer program will dictate what each output device will do. Typical output devices include: motors, bulbs, bells, buzzers, and solenoids.

This is the area most often associated with control, but it is only one aspect. The use of the computer opens up many opportunities and can extend theme work.

Control and Systems in K-3

Students should explore safely and apply control for direction, speed, and power of devices using the following:

> electrical devices
> circuits and simple switches
> output devices

Control and Systems in 4-6

Students should explore safely and apply systems to control the direction, speed, and power of devices using the following:

> electronic devices
> more elaborate switch mechanisms
> output devices
> sensors
> pulsing and counting devices
> logic gates
> simple memory systems
> computer interfaces

HUMAN ELEMENTS

In elementary school, students will be considering the human user of their designs only in a very general context. Despite this, you should keep reminding them that their designs and models need to be functional, aesthetically pleasing, and suited to the person who may be using them.

Examples that may help students better understand the concept of ergonomics include:

- There is a cupboard too high for children to reach. Design a method of taking boxes of cereal safely from this cupboard.
- There is only one table available in a room on which to place a puzzle that will take a long time to complete. The table has very short legs (only 0.5 m). Design a device that will ensure that anyone working on the puzzle will not get a sore back or neck from bending over it.

Basic Concepts

- Function concerns the use to which the system is put.
- Aesthetics are the characteristics of an object or system that appeal to a person's sense of beauty.
- Ergonomics involves the efficiency of the system in relation to work performed by the human body and mind in operating it.

Human Elements in Grades K-6

After students have created their designs, they should appreciate the following factors:

- the design should perform adequately for the required task
- appearance can be an important factor in a design.

YOUR NOTES

GETTING STARTED: MAKING YOUR OWN ACTIVITIES

Having gone through the process of thinking about what curriculum you wish to cover, the resources and space you will need, and the special needs of your students, it's time to plan the project your students will undertake. There are several activities provided in this book, ready for you to implement. However, you should view these as your "springboard" to making design and technology part of your own creative process. Here's some background that will show you both how the activities in this resource were prepared, as well as how to make your own.

Tips for Teachers New to Design and Technology

O You don't have to be an expert in this area - what is needed is the willingness to try!

O Students need opportunities to make decisions and to begin to take responsibility for their work.

O The model does not have to "be something" or "do something."

O All students need full access to all basic materials: scissors, glue, pens, crayons and other drawing materials, clay, fabric, etc.

O Give students opportunities to experiment and work with the materials.

O Show students how to use tools safely, e.g., a saw. The use of tools is not the place for experimentation!

O Put aside the urge to "straighten" a young student's gluing - it is the student's work and the student should be proud of the result.

O Let students, initially, use their own language to explain what they are doing. Technical language comes when students are ready.

O If students are interested in going further and gluing pieces of wood or card together, show them.

O Some students will want to go on to another model at the next opportunity, others will want to add more to the original work. Let students progress at their individual speeds. It is the student's decision, not yours, as to what comes next.

O Praise is especially important at the early stages of design and technology and their development in this area.

O It is extremely important that students, adult helpers, and you understand that there are no right answers in design situations. Every solution has value!

O It is essential to place students in the role of designer no matter how young they are. They must try to come up with solutions to problems. If you give a possible solution to a problem, the rest of the class will use that answer and not think creatively and independently. It is very important to let students explore and discover their own answers.

Helping Hand

You will find planning sheets to help you get started in the Appendix, starting on page 130.

The most important factor in getting started is to get started!

A Model for the Design Process

S   Situation
P   Problems, Possibilities
I   Investigation, Ideas
C   Choose, Construct
E   Evaluate

The SPICE model is a tool to help you and your students focus on the problem-solving stages of design and technology. If you are already using one of the other models that have been developed for this purpose, you will find it quite straightforward to move from SPICE to your own, and vice versa.

The design process has a very important place in your curriculum. It is fundamentally a problem-solving exercise that can be open-ended or set within certain parameters as you decide. To focus attention on the key stages, the activities in this resource were based on the following model:

- recognizing and defining the problem
- investigating the problem
- generating many ideas and possible solutions
- developing the best solutions
- creating working diagrams and models
- making the prototype
- testing the solution
- modifying the solution if not successful.

If the original solution does not work, children are encouraged to try new solutions. These ideas will come from all members of the group and build upon previous knowledge. Because of this constant flow of ideas, the design process is never static. It allows for the creation of a multitude of solutions to problems. In the design process, there is never one solution to a problem. It is this aspect that makes this approach so appropriate for children. Ideas can be tested and modified with an air of freedom and non-competitiveness. Children using this model become effective problem solvers.

The Problem-solving Approach

The problem-solving approach appears to be asking children to re-invent the wheel: why would educators want children to go through this process? The answer is that through this exploration that children will learn about their world and how to make the most of it. Attitudes and skills are developed. Children need to go through this developmental stage to develop their thought processes. This is the important "What if" aspect of design and technology.

Problem-solving is not always an entirely open-ended situation where children are left to their own devices. A problem can be presented to children for one or more specific reasons depending on the lesson objectives. Depending on these objectives, problems can be presented to the children to:

- introduce a new concept
- support the development of specific manipulative skills
- foster the appreciation for the properties of materials
- encourage the use of creative and inventive talents.

Developing a Design Problem

When developing design problems for children, it is important to start from their present stage of development and with the experiences that are central to their immediate world and environment. New learning takes place as the projects emerge from topic-based activities that are relevant to the learners.

Factors to be Considered in a Successful Design

size
cost
materials
appearance
function
ergonomics
time available
construction methods
safety
final use of product.

Children will learn to make the appropriate decisions while working through the design process.

The Design Process: An Outline

Examples of how the design process is used when developing an activity for students follow this outline.

Situation (Scenario)

The situation gives the frame of reference for the design brief or problem. This "stage setting" helps to give meaning and provides a context to the design problem posed to the children. The situation often takes into account factors such as:

○ background knowledge of the children
○ new skills or knowledge to be explored
○ availability of materials
○ use of time
○ space

Situations should be as real as possible. The situation is usually posed as a story, either true or invented. Realistic situations can be found within the home, school, and community.

These situations need to be open-ended enough to allow for a wide variety of solutions to the problem.

Helping Hand

You'll find a wide variety of sample situations in the activity section of this book. Notice how some situations are presented as visuals, such as *Puppy Protection*, page 70, while others are in a variety of text forms, ranging from classified ads to radio broadcasts (*Sweet Enterprise*, page 76, and *After the Storm*, page 88). Use whatever approach seems to grab your students' imaginations.

Problem, Possibilities (Design Brief)

The **design brief** is a short statement indicating what is to be designed and made. A detailed design brief also states any restrictions and/or requirements placed on the design such as:

- materials
- size
- cost
- time allowed
- processes to be used

    The design brief is developed in conjunction with the situation.

Investigation

During this stage of the design process, children consider different aspects of the problem. Some aspects could be:

Size
- How big (small, heavy, etc.) does it need to be to solve the problem?
- Cost
- How much money is required for this solution?

Materials
- What are the best materials for this situation?
- What materials are readily available?
- What materials need to be acquired?

Strength
- How much mass is involved?
- Will the mass always be the same?

Appearance
- What should it look like?

Functions (requirements)
- What are the main functions the design must achieve if it is to be successful?

Ergonomics
- What ergonomic features should be considered to make the design most efficient?

Safety
- What safety precautions will be needed during the construction?
- Will the design meet safety requirements?

    Students need time to investigate a wide variety of topics. Research will be required in many cases. This could involve:

- brainstorming with others in the class
- going to the library
- reading magazines and books
- talking to experts in the field
- visiting stores
- exploring similar problems and their solutions.

Helping Hand

The choice of materials can be yours or the students. If you want them to learn about the qualities of certain materials, then have only these materials available. For example, you might want them to only use newspaper and tape so that they learn how to make paper structures stronger.

Alternatively, you may want the activity to be more open ended. In that case, give the students the opportunity to work with a variety of materials including construction kits.

Ideas

Encourage children to develop a variety of ideas and possible solutions. Brainstorming is one strategy that helps children generate many thoughts. Accept all ideas. Sometimes the more far-fetched ideas lead to interesting solutions!

Children can make sketches of these preliminary ideas and concepts as they go along. Each child should have their own "design folder." Encourage children to keep all of their rough work for future reference. The folder can be helpful when working on additional activities at a later date.

Choose Idea(s) for Development

One or more of the ideas can now be expanded. Children will need to consider:

size	construction methods
desired materials	tools needed
time available	

Working Diagram or Model

A working diagram or model is now developed. A working diagram gives children the opportunity to test out their ideas before the model is actually constructed. Younger children can develop rough sketches of their ideas, although at this age level it is often easier for students to make the model first and then sketch the finished model or design. This progression allows young children to experience the more concrete aspect of the design process first before they move towards the more abstract level involving sketching. Older students should prepare a proper working diagram that indicates the dimensions of the object. The diagram should be complete enough to allow someone else to replicate the model.

A quick prototype can be constructed using material such as: Plasticine, construction paper, scrap paper, construction kits (have a wide variety available), and/or other "junk" material. This stage gives students an opportunity to see if their ideas can actually be carried out.

Construct

The product can now be constructed from the appropriate material. Children may need to learn a specific skill before the model can be constructed. It is important at this stage for children to re-examine the problem or brief to make sure that they are working towards a solution. Revisions may occur at this stage or at any other point in the process.

Evaluate

The product is tested to see if it really solves the initial problem. If the product is not satisfactory, modifications are made to the design to rectify any problem. The product is tested again. This process is continued until the children are satisfied with their results. Sometimes, they may need to return to the beginning if too many problems exist in their product.

Helping Hand

You'll find more about design folders and ongoing assessment in the discussion of Evaluation and Assessment, beginning on page 56.

Helping Hand

You will find a detailed discussion of how to help students evaluate their products on page 57 and forms to use on pages 142-3 and 150-1.

Example One - Bird Feeders

S - Situation (Scenario)

There are many birds around the schoolyard. The class likes to watch the birds feed but there is not enough food for them during the winter, and so the birds fly away. You want to be able to watch the birds all year.

P - Problem, Possibilities (Design Brief)

Create a device that allows birds to feed all year long. It must be large enough for the big birds but you do not want squirrels to get the seeds!

In this design brief, the following restrictions were included:

○ materials - must be used all year long
○ size - must accommodate the larger birds
○ location - squirrels must not be able to reach it.

I - Investigation, Ideas

Watch the birds in the yard over a period of time. Keep a record (chart) to indicate which birds come to feed at trees, plants, etc., in the area. Note the size of the birds. Look at bird feeders at home, in parks, etc. Keep a record of the kind of birds that come to certain types of feeders. This record could include the sizes of the different birds that come to the different feeders.

○ Make a list of the things needed in a bird feeder.
○ Watch the squirrels in the yard. Where can they climb?
○ What problems would this pose to the building of the feeder?
○ What alternatives could be found?
○ Develop several designs in detail.
○ Make several sketches of the models.
○ Define factors such as dimensions and availability of materials.
○ Research the types of birds in the area. Which birds migrate?

C - Choose, Construct

Select the best design that seems to fit the criteria. Develop a working diagram of the model indicating the dimensions. Construct a prototype of the design. Test the model to see if it works effectively. Make any necessary changes to the model and evaluate again. Once a design has been settled on, make the final product out of the appropriate materials.

E - Evaluate

Since the feeders are to be used by birds, the best evaluation is to put out the feeders and watch the result. Students could continue to chart the number and kind of birds that use the feeders, then compare these results to earlier records. Evaluate the feeders and make the necessary modifications. Test the new models and note any changes in frequency of birds.

The situation you provide should always draw on the interest and experience of the children. For example, most children were able to relate well to the situation on this page.

The Construct and the Evaluation component should be worked on together. Students construct a model, test it, make changes as needed, and test again. The design process is never static!

Example Two - The Desert Island

S - Situation (Scenario)

You and three members of your family have been stranded on a remote tropical island after your ship ran aground. Almost all your belongings were lost at sea. It is getting dark and it looks like it might storm. The most important thing right now is to make a shelter for the night.

P - Problem , Possibilities (Design Brief)

Design and construct a shelter for four people. It must be able to withstand the strong winds that are starting to pick up. You have little time before the storm. You have limited resources left from the ship. You do have:

a knife (scissors)
string
your research thesis (paper)

In this design brief, the following restrictions were included:

○ materials - must be able to withstand gale force winds
○ size - must accommodate four adults
○ time - only a limited amount of time is available

I - Investigation, Ideas

○ Investigate different shapes for the structures.
○ What kinds of shapes can be found in nature?
○ What shapes are present in the manufactured world?
○ What shapes withstand strong winds most effectively?
○ How are buildings in storm-affected parts of the world constructed?
○ Compare this problem with similar situations faced by campers (tents).
○ Experiment with different ways of attaching the structure to nearby vegetation or the ground, etc.
○ Make a list of the things needed to make a shelter.
○ List the essential elements for the interior of a shelter.

C - Choose, Construct

Select one idea for the shelter based on the research findings. Prepare working diagrams of the shelter based on the investigations. Construct a prototype for the shelter. Test the shelter to see if it will withstand the force of the wind (an electric fan or hair dryer). Make any modifications required and test the model again. Once a design has been settled on, make the final product using the appropriate materials.

E - Evaluate

Look at the problem and consider how well the identified requirements were achieved. Consider any possible improvements.

Activities based on Theme Work

As you think about the activities you want to use with your class, consider the broad themes that you are planning. This is an ideal cross-curricular strategy to incorporate design and technology with many areas of the curriculum and acts as a context for the learning process. Theme work also supports the learning of specific concepts. Children naturally form links in their understanding of various areas.

Encourage students to help plan the unit, perhaps through a brain-storming session. Record the answers and use these to build an initial plan. You will find out what background information the children already have and can build from there to make the activities appropriate to the needs and interests of the learners.

Prepare a series of planning charts. Use these to map out factors such as time and available resources. Keep these posted in the room during the project to help students stay on track.

You and the students will probably modify the plan as the project continues. By keeping records of the daily activities, you can adjust activities accordingly.

Activities based on Stories

Literature provides an excellent source for design and technology integration. After reading a story or a poem, challenge students to come up with solutions to problems encountered by the characters in the story.

Initially, select stories or poems that are familiar to students as sources of design briefs. In addition, use literature that revolves around curriculum topics already being studied.

Story Starter Examples

Three Billy Goats Gruff

○ The three billy goats need to find a better method of escaping from the troll. They need something strong and durable.

○ Devise an alternative system for the goats to get to the meadow. The device must be strong enough to take the mass of the biggest billy goat. Test the strength of the device using objects such as small toys or weights.

Jack and Jill

○ Jack and Jill are getting tired of going up and down that hill every day to fetch those pails of water.

○ Design an alternate method of getting the water to the bottom of the hill.

Jack and the Beanstalk

○ Jack is having trouble with his beanstalk. It is getting quite weak and hard to climb. Jack wants to be able to climb up and down it easily. He is concerned about his safety when he climbs the beanstalk.

○ Design a new climbing structure that would be safer and easier for Jack to use.

Field Trips

Field trips can support the integrated unit. Children see how things work. For example, if you are studying simple machines, take students on a field trip in the community (if possible) to see construction equipment such as front-end loaders. Find things in the community to support specific projects. If there is a new school or house in the area, use it as a basis for design work.

Current Events

Current events provide many ideas for students' investigation. Examine topics such as oil spills, deforestation of the rainforest focusing on the environment, and recycling. A topic such as the development of a school playground could be another selection. If the students select the topics, they will more likely have sustained interest.

Helping Hand

An excellent resource to help you plan any technology-related field trip is *Take a Technowalk*, from Trifolium Books. You'll find information on this and other resources starting on page 159 of the Appendix.

USING THE ACTIVITIES IN THIS BOOK

Helping Hand

Time at a premium? Look for activities that will fit into your existing plans for other curriculum topics. This will help you bring design and technology into your teaching, without sacrificing time from other subjects.

The activities in this book are organized by theme, but can be used in any combination or order that suits your needs. There is a teacher planning page and student reproducible page per activity.

These problem-solving activities have been developed in order to help you and your students understand the design process. Each one has been outlined with possible suggestions to extend or modify the project. Feel free to customize the activity to suit your class and for the technological concepts to be covered.

Recommendations

○ Encourage students to work in pairs or small groups to foster co-operation and enhance problem-solving strategies.

○ Each of the activities in this book will allow you to cover several different technological concepts. Determine which concepts could be learned through the activity. Focus on one or two major concepts rather than several. Note: Factors included under Human Elements (function, aesthetics, and ergonomics) are often covered in the activities.

Be supportive and elicit from students or remind them what they have learned in previous activities. Their technological awareness and literacy skills are built on past and present activities.

It may take quite a long time for students to grasp the concept that there are no "right or wrong" answers. Constant reinforcement and encouragement are needed.

Choosing the right activity for K-3 or 4-6

All of the activities in this book can be used in any grade, with the appropriate presentation and modification. For your planning convenience, we have selected activities that seemed particularly well-suited to younger students as "K-3." The student pages that accompany these activities are highly visual and could be handed out or used as posters over the work areas.

More Activity Ideas

Each set of activities is followed by three pages of quick activity ideas. Many of these suggest certain materials - use this as a guide only. Take into consideration factors such as age and ability level of students, previous experience, skills to be learned, etc. These are ideal activities to use as quick problem-solving exercises, in which students plan for 30 min, draw or construct for 20 min, then discuss and evaluate for 10 min. You can also use them as the starting point for more involved projects.

What You'll Find in Each Activity

Teacher Planning Page

There is a page of background, explanations, and hints with each activity. Look for these features:

○ **Synopsis** - breaks down the activity into the design model described on page 46 of this book.

○ **Starting Points** - suggests areas to consider ahead of time.

○ **Exploring** - recommendations for materials, research, and resources.

○ **Extending** - offers ideas to extend/enrich the activity for interested students (or to refresh the activity for use in subsequent years).

○ **Stimulate Further Thought by Asking** - questions you could ask while circulating in the class. They include suggestions that help students understand specific concepts. In addition, students often bring various levels of background information to the situation, and these questions will help elicit some of this information. Here are sample question starters:

"What will happen if ...?"
"How can you make it stronger/lighter/taller ... ?"
"What other materials might be suitable ... ?"
"How can you test ... ?"

The Problem

The problem stems from the situation. Depending on the activity, you may need to present the problem to your students. These problems can be presented in two different ways.

○ The more direct presentation starts with phrases such as, *"Design and create ..."* This method is more suitable for younger children or students with less experience with design and technology activities.

○ The other method is more open-ended and develops from how students see the problem. The opening question for the problem could be: *"How can this problem be solved?"*

If you wish to modify the problem, specify parameters such as:

materials	cost
resources	time allowed
size	processes and techniques to be used

The Student Page

There are a variety of student pages in this book. Some are highly visual, and are meant to suggest the situation. Use these with younger children or to encourage visual learners. Other pages contain text-supported situations, with **Think About It** questions to guide student inquiry. These pages include a self-assessment chart students can complete when finished the project. See the Assessment section on page 63 for more details on how to use these charts.

Helping Hand

In the activities in this book, a more directed approach has been adopted to help you get started. Feel free to modify the activities and materials as needed to make it more meaningful for your students.

Helping Hand

With younger, or less experienced designers, it is helpful to assign specific types and quantities of materials to the task. If such students are given free choice for the material selection, they often don't choose wisely initially or are unable to decide what materials would be most suitable for the situation.

EVALUATION AND ASSESSMENT

Helping Hand

In this book, and other design & technology resources, evaluation refers to testing of the product against the parameters set by the problem.

Evaluation has a very specific meaning when used in design and technology. It refers to the testing of the product, whether design, model, or prototype. Evaluation is done continuously throughout the activity, and is used to indicate where changes would improve the product. As you and your students work through the activities in this book, you will find reminders of the key areas to evaluate for each project.

Evaluation and Your Students

There are three main areas to consider when planning how evaluation will take place.

1. Students should evaluate their work using a specific set of criteria. These criteria are simply the factors that were considered to be important in the problem, such as protection from the sun and wind in the activity Puppy Protection.
2. Students should have the opportunity to evaluate the work of others using the same specific set of criteria. It is immensely valuable to learn that there are no "wrong" answers, just different solutions that may or may not work well. This is the time to emphasize constructive criticism as well as the sharing of ideas.
3. Students should maintain some type of ongoing record, such as the design folder described below, in order to track their progress through the activity. For example, if a model bridge was evaluated and found to need strengthening, the student should record both the test and the change to the design.

The Design Folder

A design folder is a large envelope or file folder used by students to store their working drawings and ideas for one or more projects. They should record all changes they make and the reasons why each change was necessary. You can use the folder as part of your assessment as well as to track why a student chose a particular solution to the design problem.

If you are doing short, problem-solving activities with the students, each problem and its design solution can be stored in the folder. After doing a few activities, have students review their work. They will begin to see a pattern in the approaches that led to successful solutions.

If you are doing longer term projects, with research components and working prototypes, the design folder will be an invaluable aid to help keep students on task and organized.

Evaluating Students' Designs

Example: Evaluating a Vehicle

Each model can be tested and evaluated on criteria such as: distance travelled, speed attained, design improvements, and safety. A fun way to do this is to stage a competition where all students agree on a test, or construct a track, and then test the vehicles' performance. Make sure that there is time for discussion after the competition and that students appreciate the design features that contributed to the success of the vehicles that performed well.

Example: Evaluating a Load-bearing Structure

A successful structure will resist buckling and will not fall over easily. Mass can be added in increments to each model until they collapse (testing to destruction) or are moved a specific amount (deflection). Students can use the results to calculate a ratio that represents the strength of each structure as follows: **Ratio = maximum load supported / mass of structure.**

Example: Evaluating a New Invention

Some activities are intended to encourage students to exercise their imaginations by inventing some new technology. While you and your class may decide on a creative way to test or evaluate such a design, you may want to try this approach instead, especially if you are facing a class full of unrelated yet very interesting projects. Evaluate each student's or group's work on the basis of presentation. Does the design seem well-thought out? Has the student considered several factors in the design? What is the response of other students to the design? Has the student/group followed all of the steps of the design process, that is, from situation to evaluation?

Something to Ponder

It may take time for your students to become comfortable with the idea that there is no one right answer to any design problem. It may also take time for them to stop resisting the idea of modifying their work once it is "done." Yet these are the realities of many aspects of the everyday world. Point out improvements to technology they are familiar with, such as electronic games or telephones. If you have both a modern and an older grocery store in your area, why not take students on a field trip to experience the changes in the checkout process?

Once you and your students are familiar with the design process, you will notice the noise level rising. Students will take risks in the comfort of knowing that there are many possible solutions. They will discuss ideas and share skills. They will learn to accept difficulties as challenges. Your only problem may be in getting them to stop!

Helping Hand

When evaluating a load-bearing structure, you should consider your students' feelings about their work. Testing to destruction is fine for some students but can be upsetting to others -- especially younger designers who are very proud of their product.

Assessment

Consider this area carefully, especially when you first start your design and technology program. For example, what outcomes in terms of skills, knowledge, and attitudes do you want to make sure are developed?

A topic web is useful here. Initially, parents and senior administration may be unclear about "what the children are learning." Spend time on these areas now to reduce frustration later!

As you know, assessment is ideally an on-going process that provides continual feedback to students to enhance their learning. In today's dynamic classroom environment, teachers are looking for a variety of authentic ways to assess student learning and achievement. Educators want tools which can help them acquire specific information about student performance. Students also want to know the criteria which will be used to assess the final products they develop and the tasks they perform.

Rubrics are one of many methods used to collect data which allow educators to make judgments about student performance. We have included the following discussion about using rubrics for authentic assessment for those teachers who may be unfamiliar with them. Rubrics can be developed by teachers and students alike.

Authentic Assessment using Rubrics

Rubrics are an ideal learning and assessment tool that can also help clarify expectations for students, teachers, and parents. A rubric may look like a checklist but it does more than merely identify work that needs to be done by the student. Rubrics clarify the expected standards for doing a good job and encourage self-assessment by the student.

The Checklist Rubric

This type is usually used to define the standards of excellence for the student. Often a "yes" or "no" can be checked off to indicate whether the standard has been met by the student or group being evaluated. These are usually the easiest types for you and your students to familiarize yourselves with as you begin to experiment with rubrics. A sample is provided on page 60.

The Scored Rubric

This type of rubric rates the level of performance of the student in working toward a high standard of achievement. In other words, instead of simply checking off whether or not students have met the criteria set out, a judgment is made about the quality of the product or performance. A sample is provided on page 60.

Helping Hand

If you are familiar with rubrics and their use, please skip this introductory material and go to page 60. You'll find an activity to help your students' develop their own rubrics for self-assessment.

How Rubrics Are Used

You can apply rubrics to a variety of subject areas across the curriculum, or gear them to a specific subject or task/performance within a discipline.

Rubrics can be used to support outcomes-based learning as an assessment tool and can be aligned to essential learner outcomes and specific program outcomes. They may be used throughout an outcomes-based unit or can be designed for the culminating activity. We recommend that you and your students become familiar with rubrics before letting students design their own. You may want to develop a rubric with your entire class as part of the familiarization process. This will allow students to have input on the criteria being established and provide them with an opportunity to think about all the elements of a particular task or performance. This is also an ideal way for students to gain insight into how assessment and evaluation are conducted.

The Benefits

Rubrics provide specific feedback to the learner from a variety of sources. Teachers, students, peers, and parents may all use rubrics to assess learning and evaluate the quality of student products/performance. Students are often the best judge of their own performance, knowing their personal strengths and weaknesses. Rubrics are a concrete way for them to identify what they did well and what they need to improve on. Peers can also provide constructive feedback, perhaps because they've gone through a similar learning process or experience. Students value their peers' input and appreciate receiving positive reinforcement from them. Teachers and parents are also essential in the assessment process using rubrics to assist with areas of difficulty while guiding the learner to higher levels of achievement.

Developing Rubrics of Your Own

When designing rubrics keep in mind the following guidelines:

○ choose a specific learning focus for the rubric, making sure all criteria supports the focus
○ write ideas in statement form with simple language
○ use "I" and "we" pronouns to personalize the criteria for students
○ use descriptive verbs in all rubric statements
○ choose criteria that reflect a high standard of achievement
○ select criteria that seems attainable to students
○ order the criteria in a logical sequence that reflects the learning process
○ use sub-headings throughout the rubric if criteria can be grouped
○ use graphics to make your rubric attractive to students.

Use the sample rubrics on the following pages to guide you as you make your own.

Helping Hand

If you want to create a "scored rubric," which judges how well a product or performance was done, simply change yes/no columns to a series of headings like :

4 superior

3 proficient

2 competent

1 needs improvement

Put the mark (number) in the appropriate column and tally the marks at the bottom of the page to see how well your group did.

Activity - Rubrics Rule!

PART 1 - Learning About Rubrics

Rubrics are checklists that can help you understand the standards that are expected when you perform a task or create a product. They also allow you to assess your own and others' performances.

What to Do

Look at each of the sample rubrics prepared for another class. Answer the following questions about each rubric, then prepare one yourself.

1. What is the focus of the rubric?
2. Does the rubric focus on something being produced or a performance?
3. Where could you use this rubric in your studies?
4. Rubrics should describe how a person or group did something. Does this rubric focus on a person or a group?
5. Who is able to assess the student's performance using the rubric?

Sample Rubric #1

Rubric Focus: Working in a Group

Student Name: Cara Smith
Names of Partners: Hakim Rashid, Sasha Zytes
Peer Evaluators: Kathy Clark, Tim Sullivan

CRITERIA	SELF	PEER	TEACHER
I performed my assigned role.	(yes)/no	(yes)/no	(yes)/no
I stayed on task.	(yes)/no	yes /(no)	yes/(no)
I did my fair share of the work.	(yes)/no	(yes)/no	yes/(no)
I listened to others' ideas.	yes/(no)	yes /(no)	yes/(no)
I helped the group solve problems.	(yes)/no	yes /(no)	(yes)/ no
I completed my work on time.	(yes)/no	(yes)/no	(yes)/ no

Sample Rubric #2

Rubric Focus : Making a Visual Display

Student Names: Michelle Leblanc, Forrest Chambers, Jim Powel
Evaluators: Cindy Kramer, Ali Tamar

CRITERIA	GROUP	PEER	TEACHER
We developed a plan for our display.	0 1 2 3 4 (5)	0 1 2 3 4 (5)	0 1 2 3 4 (5)
We targeted our display to an audience.	0 1 2 3 4 (5)	0 1 2 3 4 (5)	0 1 2 3 4 (5)
We arranged our information in a logical sequence.	0 1 2 3 (4) 5	0 1 2 3 (4) 5	0 1 2 3 (4) 5
We included both information and graphics.	0 1 (2) 3 4 5	0 1 2 (3) 4 5	0 1 2 (3) 4 5
We used bold headings and titles.	0 1 2 (3) 4 5	0 1 2 (3) 4 5	0 1 2 (3) 4 5
We highlighted important concepts.	0 1 2 3 4 (5)	0 1 2 3 (4) 5	0 1 2 3 (4) 5

Note: 0 is incomplete; 3 is a good effort; 5 is an outstanding effort.

Adapted with permission from Career Connections *Teacher Resource Bank III* Copyright Trifolium Books Inc. & Weigl Educational Publishers.

Part 2 - Try Your Own Rubric

Now it's your turn to create a rubric. Use the ideas below to develop rubric statements for keeping a good notebook. Try to use powerful, active words (verbs) to express your ideas and the right pronoun ("I") for this type of rubric. Arrange the statements in a rubric outline like the samples provided.

Example of rubric statement:

○ neatness - *I wrote neatly in my notebook.*

○ organization-

○ complete notes-

○ wise use of space-

○ titles/dates included-

○ underlined headings-

○ legible handwriting-

○ add your own ideas-

Rubric Focus: A Good Notebook

Student Name: _____

Names of Partners: _____

Peer Evaluators: _____

Use the rubric to evaluate one of your own notebooks. Put a check mark in the yes/no column that corresponds with each criteria. When you are finished have your partner do a peer evaluation and compare your results.

Activity - A Design and Technology Presentation Rubric

As you work on your project, discuss with your partner/group how you will present your final product to the class. Brainstorm a list of ideas for your presentation.

1. Discuss what makes a good presentation. Make a chart like the one below. List your ideas under the following headings:

Presentation	Organization	Content (product/model)	Report
_____	_____	_____	_____
_____	_____	_____	_____
_____	_____	_____	_____

2. You may wish to add headings of your own or change them according to the specific requirements of your project.

3. Put a star* beside 10 to 12 of the most important ideas that you would like to include in your rubric.

4. Put the ideas in a logical order, numbering them from 1-10/12, and keeping them grouped with similar ideas.

5. Turn your ideas into rubric statements, following the rubric guidelines developed in the previous activity.

6. Look at how your statements are ordered/grouped. If you wish to include sub-headings for each grouping, think of an appropriate name.

7. Now produce a finished version of your rubric by writing the statements (and headings) into an outline. (If you wish, use a desktop publishing package which may be available to you.)

8. Decide who will evaluate the criteria you've selected (self/peer/teacher) and include this on your rubric outline.

9. Make sure you've stated the rubric focus at the top of your rubric.

When you've finished preparing for your presentation, do a trial run of the presentation for your group. Test the rubric by having the group do a self-evaluation. Make any changes that you feel are necessary.

Self- and Peer Assessment

An on-going self-assessment will help your students' monitor their own progress. They will be able to recognize their own strengths and where they need to focus more effort. In this book, forms and charts have been provided that students can complete and keep in their design folder.

Here are some suggestions to help you and your students obtain the maximum benefit from self- and peer assessment.

Helping Hand
You will find self- and peer assessment forms in the Appendix, starting on page 152.

❍ Students who are not accustomed to self-assessment may be uncomfortable giving themselves the "credit" they are due. It can help if you suggest they complete the form as if a close friend or family member was assessing their work.

❍ Ensure that students appreciate the value of the assessment. One way is to review the past few assessments on a regular basis. Discuss with the student any changes or patterns that may appear.

❍ If you wish, add a ranking system to the assessment and have students add up their score over several projects.

❍ When students assess each other, there may at first be a tendency to be overly generous. Assure them that honest criticism and assessment will be a greater benefit in the long run. (Watch for discrepancies between self- and peer assessment. It can help indicate when students do not quite grasp the importance of honest assessment.)

❍ Younger students can provide more detailed assessment with the help of an adult or older student to record their responses.

Other Forms of Assessment

Some assorted strategies you can use to assess different aspects of a student's work include:

❍ observational checklists (rubrics)
❍ group work
❍ informal and formal conferencing
❍ written work
❍ presentation skills - oral, project
❍ formal evaluation

Helping Hand

You will find an assessment form based on these attributes on page 144 of the Appendix.

For Young Students

Different strategies are required to assess young children's progress in design and technology activities. The major question to ask is "How has design and technology contributed to the students' development?" This question can focus on the following attributes:

confidence	creativity
imagination	flexibility
practical skills	reasoning ability
organization	co-operation
leadership	planning ability
manual dexterity	motivation
attitudes	language skills
mathematical skills	hand-eye co-ordination

Let the magic begin!

ANIMAL SHELTERS

Overview of Activities

Activity	Recommended for Grades*	Project	Recommended Materials	Advance Preparation
Adopt a Bear	4-6	Design a bear enclosure for a zoo.	Found materials, wood, construction kits	Schedule research time in the library or using computer search. *Optional*: combine with a visit to a local zoo or park.
Puppy Protection	K-3	Make a shelter from wind and sun for a puppy.	Found materials; wood; plasticine;	*Optional*: arrange a class visit with a puppy and its owner.
Hop Along Home	4-6	Design a rabbit hutch to hold an expanding number of rabbits.	Cardboard; plastic mesh or cheesecloth; popsicle sticks and other found materials; sand, etc. *Optional*: Computer drawing software	Schedule research time in the library or using computer search. *Optional*: arrange to visit a rabbitry and interview the farmer.
A Safe Place	K-3	Make a temporary home for an animal visitor.	Found materials; plastic pop bottles; natural materials.ie. dry grass or sticks	*Optional*: begin with a "model animal" research project.
Sweet Enterprise	4-6	Design an artificial beehive.	Cardboard tubes and other found materials; samples of geometric shapes.	*Optional*: arrange a visit from a beekeeper; arrange a visit to a local farmers' market

* This recommendation is based solely on the reading level of the student worksheets provided for each activity. Any of these activities could be used successfully with students from K-6 with appropriate presentation and support.

What is the technology in...

Here are sample webs related to the topic of animal shelters to help you get started. There are many possible entries and links which could be made. In the webs on these two pages, the distinction is made between animal shelters that are found or are part of the animal's body and those shelters that are constructed (built) in some fashion. With your students, develop webs like these to generate and record ideas. Post the web(s) in the class as a reminder.

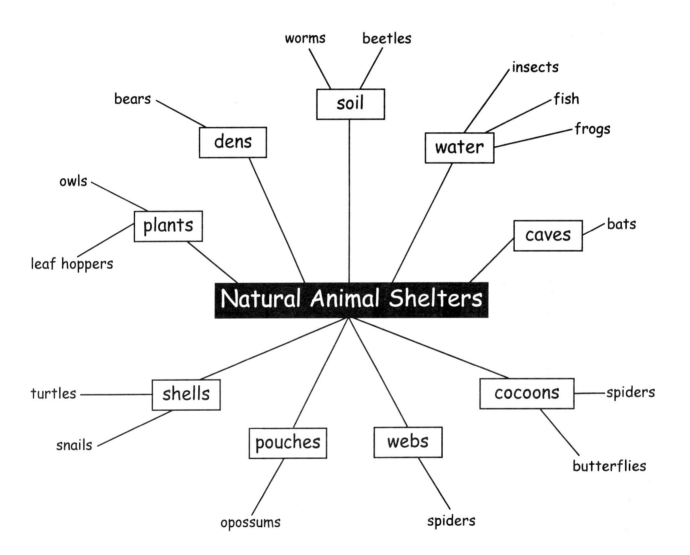

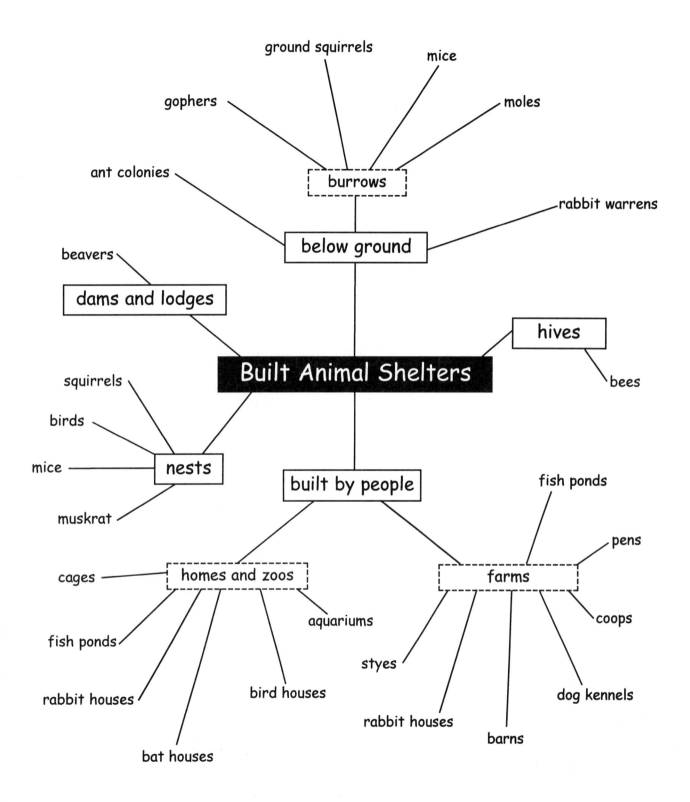

Built Animal Shelters

below ground
- ground squirrels
- mice
- moles
- gophers
- ant colonies
- rabbit warrens

via burrows

dams and lodges
- beavers

hives
- bees

nests
- squirrels
- birds
- mice
- muskrat

built by people

homes and zoos
- cages
- fish ponds
- rabbit houses
- bat houses
- bird houses
- aquariums

farms
- fish ponds
- pens
- coops
- dog kennels
- barns
- rabbit houses
- styes

Teacher Planning for *Adopt a Bear*

The school has contributed to the fundraising efforts of the local zoo to help build an enclosure for an orphaned black bear. In gratitude for the students' interest, the zoo has asked for their participation in the design and planning of the enclosure, based on the needs of the bear and other considerations.

Synopsis

Situation: Orphaned cub arriving at local zoo.

Problem: Need to build a new bear compound. Students asked for design ideas.

Investigation: Life history of black bears; natural and made shelters; construction materials.

Construction: Drawn and written project; extend to scale models.

Evaluation: How well does each design serve the three clients involved: the bear, the zookeepers, and the viewing public?

Starting Points

○ What information will be needed about bears to make sure all factors have been included in the designs?

Exploring

○ Conduct research to learn about the natural habitats of bears.

○ Find out the size of a fully grown black bear (especially its mass.)

○ Experiment with different materials to find which ones provide the most strength.

Extending

○ The zookeepers need to contain the bear while cleaning the open area.

○ One section of the shelter is to be built on an island surrounded by a moat. Consider how the bear will travel across the water to get to this part of the compound.

○ The area must accommodate two bears that sometimes need separate shelters.

Helping Hand

Use the web, "Built Animal Shelters" page 67.

Stimulate Further Thought by Asking:

○ How does the design incorporate the natural landscape of the black bear's environment?

○ How are zoo visitors able to view the bear when it is either outside or inside?

○ What precautions will ensure that visitors will not throw any objects into the bear's compound?

More Activity Ideas

Finding the Strongest Structure, pg 78

Stable Platform, pg 78

Breaking Down Walls, pg 78

The Channel Bridge, pg 78

The Flexible Bridge, pg 79

Animal Traps, pg 79

The Simple Bridge, pg 126

Adopt a Bear

Your school has helped to raise money so the local zoo could care for an orphaned young black bear. Enough money has been raised and now the zoo is ready to design and build the new compound where the bear will live. The zookeepers have written the following letter to your school.

To the students:

Thank you for your work in helping to raise money for our new bear compound. Because of your interest in this project, we would like to give you the chance to help design the compound. Here is a list of the important features that should be included in your design. Don't forget: the cub is very small now, but it will grow quickly into a large and powerful bear.

Features

The bear will need a shelter for its winter sleep.

There must be space for the bear to roam about and exercise freely.

The bear should have an interesting environment that will keep it active and entertained.

It should be easy for visitors to the zoo to watch the bear without disturbing it.

The compound should be aesthetically pleasing: that is, it should look good in the zoo!

Yours truly,
The zookeepers

Think About It

1. What information do you need before you can start your design?
2. How big should the shelter be?
3. What materials would work the best? How will you decide?
4. The compound will have an outside area and a shelter. How could you make a door to the shelter that lets the bear move freely in and out?
5. How will you present your design?
6. How can you use the computer to record your work?

Circle your choice for this project.

1. I worked well with others.

Always   Sometimes   Not Often

2. I tried different ideas.

Always   Sometimes   Not Often

3. I did my best.

Always   Sometimes   Not Often

4. I feel this way about my accomplishment:

_____

Synopsis

Situation: A new puppy needs care.

Problem: No shelter or shade available in backyard.

Investigation: Climate; needs of a young animal; how animals grow; strength of structures.

Construction: Model, to scale or not, or a full-sized prototype of cardboard.

Evaluation: How well does each design meet the specifications of protection from wind and sun? Test the shelter using a fan or hair blower (wind) and using a flashlight (sunshine).

Helping Hand

Use the web, " Built Animal Shelters" page 67.

More Activity Ideas

Finding the Strongest Structure, pg 78

Breaking Down Walls, pg 78

Drawbridge, pg 79

Animal Traps, pg 79

Flagpole, pg 80

Teacher Planning for *Puppy Protection*

Maria's parents are finally going to let her have a puppy. She wants to take good care of it. She has a backyard with a good fence, so the dog will be able to get fresh air and exercise even when she is busy. But there isn't any shelter or shade in her yard. Where will Maria's puppy rest out of the sun or wind? Design a suitable outdoor shelter for her new pet. It should look nice enough to have in a backyard, but be sturdy and safe for the puppy to use – even after it grows up.

Starting Points

○ You may wish to have students design and build a shelter for a stuffed toy. This allows evaluation in the classroom using a fan and flashlight.

○ What type of dog is going to use the shelter? How will the characteristics of this dog affect the design?

○ What materials for your model can be chosen to represent those used in a real dog house?

○ Is there a parent or classroom volunteer who could bring in a puppy and discuss dog ownership? (Check on your school policy regarding animal visits as well as any allergy concerns. Alternative: visit a local animal shelter or a kennel.)

Exploring

○ Find out about the sizes of different dogs.

○ Examine commercially-built dog houses.

○ Work with different materials to determine their durability and strength.

Extending

○ How could you decorate the puppy shelter? (It can be especially rewarding to offer students an unusual goal, such as shapes that would suit a Japanese Garden.)

○ Design a door that closes automatically when the dog goes into its house.

○ The puppy will grow quite large. Include this in your design.

Stimulate Further Thought by Asking:

○ What weather conditions need to be considered during the rest of the year?

○ How well would your shelter protect the puppy from rain, mosquitoes, or other animals? What could be added to make it better protection?

○ How could the door on the dog house be controlled by an electronic switch or a computer?

Puppy Protection

Synopsis

Situation: Rabbit shelter is too small to allow for increasing numbers.

Problem: Design a system that will house rabbits and allow for increasing numbers.

Investigation: Life history of rabbits; care of living things; natural and built environments

Construction: Computer-generated drawing of system; could extend to a physical model.

Evaluation: How easily can more animals be accommodated by the system?

Helping Hand

Use the web, "Built Animal Shelters" page 67.

More Activity Ideas

Breaking Down Walls, pg 78

Flagpole, pg 80

Super Structures, pg 110

The Geodesic Dome, pg 126

Teacher Planning for *Hop Along Home*

You are the owner of a rabbit farm and raise rabbits to sell to pet shops. You want to be able to increase the number of rabbits you can raise, but your present breeding and shelter premises are too small.

Starting Points

- What field trips will help students understand animal housing needs?
- How can parent volunteers, local pet store owners, and/or community helpers be involved in this project? You may also be able to obtain help from student peers with computer drawing software.
- What materials are readily available for this project?

Exploring

- Learn about the habits of rabbits.
- Find out about rabbit warrens. (Note: different species of rabbit have different habits. Some, including many pet varieties, are solitary.)
- Experiment with structures to find methods of adding strength without adding mass to an object.

Extending

- Make a shelter to house a mother and her newborn baby rabbits.
- Design a method to record the growth of rabbits on a regular basis.
- Some kinds of rabbits prefer shelters hidden underground. Consider including an underground area in your design.

Stimulate Further Thought by Asking:

- How will the rabbits be fed?
- How will you ensure that each rabbit will get its fair share of food?
- Rabbits are able to chew through wood and to burrow underground. What precautions will you consider to make sure that the rabbits will not escape? What materials will be used to prevent escape?

Hop Along Home

You are the owner of a small rabbitry (rabbit farm). You raise rabbits to sell to pet shops. This year, there is a greater demand for these pets than in previous years. You'd like to increase the number of rabbits you can raise. The only problem is that your rabbit breeding and shelter area has no room for more animals. You need a new system that will allow you to add more rabbits easily.

What kind of additional shelter can you design that would provide a safe habitat for more rabbits? Remember, rabbits breed quickly and this should be taken into account in the design plans. The rabbits need to move about freely but also need protection from natural enemies and bad weather.

RABBITS WANTED

SPEAK TO THE MANAGER

TOP DOLLAR FOR HEALTHY PET STOCK

Think About It

1. Where can information about rabbits be found?
2. How many offspring do rabbits produce at one time? How will this affect the design?
3. How will you test your design?
4. How many tests will be required to find the best model for the situation?
5. Is this a project that can be worked through alone or will a team be better? Why?
6. Will reviewing the problem with other people be helpful?

Circle your choice for this project.

1. I worked well with others.

Always   Sometimes   Not Often

2. I tried different ideas.

Always   Sometimes   Not Often

3. I did my best.

Always   Sometimes   Not Often

4. I feel this way about my accomplishment:

_____

Synopsis

Situation: A small wild animal has been brought to school and cannot be returned for several hours.

Problem: Need to make a temporary shelter to safely house the animal.

Investigation: Life history of the animal; natural shelters; care of living things.

Construction: Drawing and/or full-sized prototype.

Evaluation: How well will the shelter keep the animal safe during its visit? How well can the animal be observed without disturbance?

Helping Hand

Use the web, "Built Animal Shelters" page 67.

More Activity Ideas

Drawbridge, pg 79
Jack and Jill, pg 94
Hidden Treasure, pg 110
Lifting Device, pg 110

Teacher Planning Page for *A Safe Place*

Even if they have been told not to handle wild animals, younger students will often present their teacher with some living treasure found on the way to school. The trick is to find a safe place to house the earthworm, frog, or insect until it can be returned to its natural surroundings at the end of the day. This is an ideal opportunity to explore what animals require for safety and shelter – and can turn out to be a very practical exercise as well!

Starting Points

- ❍ If you wish, pick a specific animal that must be cared for, such as a butterfly and have students make a model animal to use. Or have student groups decide on the animal they want to research.
- ❍ Help students understand why the animal must be returned to its habitat.
- ❍ What information will be needed about caring for animals?
- ❍ Elicit from students what a temporary shelter should provide, such as protection, privacy, fresh air, water, a place to rest, etc. E.g. a flying animal needs a perch; a burrowing animal needs material to hide under. Students could also consider how to help the animal keep clean.
- ❍ The shelter should have a means of observing the animal.
- ❍ How big must the temporary shelter be? Which materials can be used?
- ❍ What adhesive materials can be tested for strength and durability?

Exploring

- ❍ Talk to a local conservation group or other animal protection agencies about the proper treatment of wild animals. Invite a speaker to the class.
- ❍ Investigate various types of insects to determine their needs.
- ❍ Visit a pet shop or zoo to observe small animal shelters.

Extending

- ❍ Devise a method of recording the activity of the animal.
- ❍ Alter the shelter's design so it could be used to house several small animals (such as insects or earthworms) for a few weeks.
- ❍ What type of shelter would an aquatic animal need besides water?

Stimulate Further Thought By Asking:

- ❍ How has the design been tested to meet the criteria of safety, comfort, and durability?
- ❍ How safely can the shelter be carried with the animal inside?
- ❍ How can you determine if your temporary shelter is similar to the natural home of the animal?

A Safe Place

Synopsis

Situation: An opportunity to sell honey.

Problem: Need a place to keep bees.

Investigation: Honeybees; Beekeeping; Geometric Shapes

Construction: Model of a section of the hive; computer-generated drawings; Students could use a variety of construction kits and materials to construct a prototype.

Evaluation: What is the maximum number of bees per volume (assuming one bee/cell)? Other evaluation factors include: accessibility of honey, protection of the queen from disturbance, and weather proofing.

Helping Hand

Use the web, "Natural Animal Shelters" page 66.

More Activity Ideas

Teacher Planning Page for *Sweet Enterprise*

You live on a small farm and contribute to the family chores, looking after livestock and maintaining equipment. You decide you want to raise money with an enterprise of your own. You have always been interested in raising animals. When you check the newspaper, you notice that there is space available at the local farmer's market. You decide to raise bees and to sell honey at the market.

Starting Points

- Review or introduce geometric shapes prior to this assignment.
- What are the best geometric shapes for structures?
- What construction kits will be most suitable for this activity?
- How will the different containers be tested to determine which one will hold a large bee population, thus ensuring a good honey supply?

Exploring

- Who can be invited to the class to provide background information?
- Find out about natural bee hives.
- Experiment with different shapes to see which is the strongest and most suitable for the container.

Extending

- Design a tool that will remove the honey and yet keep you safe from the bees.
- Adapt the container to allow for the addition of more bees.
- Consider the aesthetic qualities of the container.

Stimulate Further Thought by Asking:

- How can you ensure that the queen bee will not be disturbed when you extract honey?
- What methods of recording the production levels of the honey will you consider?
- How can your container be moved safely to different areas?
- If you live in an area with cold winters, how could you modify your design to help protect the bees from the change in temperature?

SWEET ENTERPRISE

You live on a small farm and help your family with the everyday chores. One day you decide you would like to find a way to earn some extra money for yourself and your family. When reading the local paper, you notice the following ad. The farm fields have lots of nectar-filled flowers — so you decide to raise bees and to sell honey.

Design a container that will allow the bees to live as naturally as possible. Remember, you must be able to remove the honey safely. The shelter will be outside so it must be able to withstand the various weather conditions.

NOW AVAILABLE..

Space for New Vendors at L & J's Farmers' Market!

Reasonable Rates; Canopies and Parking Supplied

Sell your fresh produce, preserves, honey, or custom crafts every Saturday morning. Be your own boss!

Call Linda or Jerry at 555-1234 to reserve your table today!

Think About It

1. What are the key elements of a natural hive?
2. What information will you need before you start designing?
3. What materials are best for this project?
4. How will sketching be helpful in this activity?
5. How can the different materials be tested to determine the best shape to house bees and the honey they produce?

Circle your choice for this project.

1. I worked well with others.

Always   Sometimes   Not Often

2. I tried different ideas.

Always   Sometimes   Not Often

3. I did my best.

Always   Sometimes   Not Often

4. I feel this way about my accomplishment:

More Activity Ideas

Finding the Strongest Structure

Recommended Materials: popsicle sticks or strips of heavy card, hole punch, paper fasteners, LEGO or other construction kits

The owner of a construction company has progressive design ideas for houses. She wants to design new shapes for living quarters. She wants to test the strengths of materials and shapes before she orders new equipment and supplies. Construct different shapes out of the materials. Which shape provides the strongest structure? Which design uses the least amount of material, yet provides the strongest shape?

○ What is the largest structure that you can build?

○ What is the best way to join shapes together?

○ How can you test the structures to determine the strongest shape?

○ Where can you find examples of triangular structures around you?

Stable Platform

Recommended Materials: 1 sheet thin card, 3 sheets of plain paper, masking tape, weights

The observation tower at the Island Airport is experiencing technical difficulties. An engineer must be able to work on the top of this tower. A platform is needed that will support the mass of this person. Build a model of a free standing structure with a platform capable of supporting the mass of a person. It should be as high as possible.

○ What happens if you fold the paper differently?

○ How does the size of the platform affect the stability of the tower?

○ What can be added to the platform to make it easier for the person to stand on top of the structure?

Breaking Down Walls

Recommended Materials: bricks made from paper cubes (Equilateral Shapes), construction kits (Lasy, LEGO, etc.), paper cups, bottle tops, flower pots, paper tubes, marshmallows (anything that can be stacked can be used as walls)

You have just moved into a new neighbourhood high on a hill that is often very windy. You want to protect your home by constructing a wall around the garden. Design a variety of ways to construct walls.

○ What different patterns can you use for laying down the bricks - vertical layers, etc.?

○ What ways can you use to test the strength of the different walls?

○ Which material and pattern is the strongest?

The Channel Bridge

Recommended Materials: 5 sheets of 8 1/2 x 14 paper, tape, scissors, model cars or trucks (to test the strength)

Sometimes you drive to Anytown with your family. When you do that, you cross a bridge. The bridge cannot carry too great a mass anymore. Cars are very heavy! Design a model bridge that will be able to carry heavy cars and trucks. The bridge needs to span a gap of two m. The structure must support as much mass as possible.

○ What happens if you bend the paper?

○ How does a variation in the height affect the design?

○ What combinations can be used to add strength?

The Flexible Bridge

Recommended Materials: paper clips, straws, string, Plasticine

A bridge crosses a river in the park close to school. It is a suspension bridge. You want to get a better understanding of how this type of bridge works. Design a model suspension bridge for the park. Make a bridge using straws and paper clips only. The bridge should support as great a mass as possible.

○ How can you test the strength of the bridge?

○ How can you bend the paper clips to be used for this bridge?

○ What can you do to the straws to add strength to the bridge?

Animal Traps

Recommended Materials: Any (Hint: think about weights, springs, levers, and the effects of gravity)

You are a zoologist studying endangered species. You are deep in the jungle when you come across an injured animal. Because this animal is so rare, you decide to capture it in order to protect it from predators until it is healthy. Construct an enclosure that traps the animal inside and keeps it safe from predators.

The Lunar Shelter

Recommended Materials: 1 sheet of paper, 1 marble, 3 centicubes, ruler, masking tape, etc.

Construct a shelter that could withstand the force of a meteorite (represented by a marble) falling from a height of 20 cm. A stick of 3 centicubes inside the shelter must not be knocked over by the force of the impact. (Control extension: the shelter sounds an alarm when the object it contains falls over.)

Drawbridge

Recommended Materials: 2 sheets of thin card, thin string, 3 bricks or blocks, scissors

You live in early times in a fort surrounded by water. At night, the drawbridge is raised to keep those inside safe from the world outside In the morning, the drawbridge is lowered so you and the others can go and tend the fields. Design a model of a drawbridge that is operational from the inside of the fort. It must be strong enough to take the horses and carts that use it.

○ What happens if the length of the drawbridge is increased?

○ How can you make the bridge open from both directions?

○ How can the entrance be attached to front walls?

The Daily News

Recommended Materials: 2 sheets of newspaper, 1 m of string, electric fan or hair dryer for testing the structure

You and your friend wonder if you can live in the wilds for a few days with as few of life's "necessities" as possible. You pack up your gear and set off. Unfortunately, a storm comes out of the north. You must build yourself a shelter for the evening. The only possible item of use are the maps you brought along with you. Make a model of the shelter. The shelter must be able to withstand the forces of very strong wind. There are no trees or structures near by, so the shelter will need to be self-supporting. It must be large enough for you and your friend.

○ How can you make the structure large enough to get inside?

○ What can you do to keep the shelter from falling over?

○ Which shapes are the weakest? the strongest?

○ How can you roll the newspaper to create tubular shapes?

○ How does changing the diameter of the newspaper tube affect its strength?

Flagpole

Recommended Materials: 4 sheets of newspaper, masking tape, scissors, electric fan or hair dryer for testing the structure

You live in a very windy area. You would like to put up a flagpole but you are worried that it might be blown over. A special new design is needed. Design and construct a structure that will reach out as far as possible from a fixed point and remain stable. The structure must be able to withstand a strong wind.

○ How tall/long can you make the structure?

○ What is the least amount of newspaper you can use?

○ How can you design the structure to use the least amount of tape?

YOUR NOTES

Overview of Activities

Activity	Recommended for Grades*	Project	Recommended Materials	Advance Preparation
Helpful Breezes	4-6	Design a device that uses wind power to carry a load.	Found materials; wood; construction kits; plastic bottles.	*Optional*: bring in an assortment of wind-powered devices.
Weather Watch	K-3	Design a weather monitoring device.	Found materials; wood; construction kits.	Arrange an outdoor location for student devices to be used. *Optional*: arrange Internet access for student research.
After the Storm	4-6	Design an emergency shelter for a family.	Found materials; popsicle sticks; wood; fabric. other	Schedule research time in the library or using computer search. *Optional*: arrange to visit an outdoors store to examine tents.
Winter Games	K-3	Make a game that could be outdoors.	Found materials; plastic pop bottles; sports equipment. dry grass or sticks	*Optional*: evaluate during a school play day.
Energize!	4-6	Design an energy system for a home, based on wind, water, or solar energy.	Cardboard tubes and other found materials; foil; *optional:* circuits.	Schedule research time in the library or using computer search. *Optional*: arrange to visit a solar home.

*This recommendation is based solely on the reading level of the student worksheets provided for each activity. Any of these activities could be used successfully with students from K-6 with appropriate presentation and support.

What is the technology in...

Here are sample webs related to the topic of weather to help you get started. There are many possible entries and links which could be made. In the webs on these two pages, the distinction is made between observing the weather and using weather-related phenomenon as sources of energy.

With your students, develop webs like these to generate and record ideas. Post the web(s) in the class as a reminder.

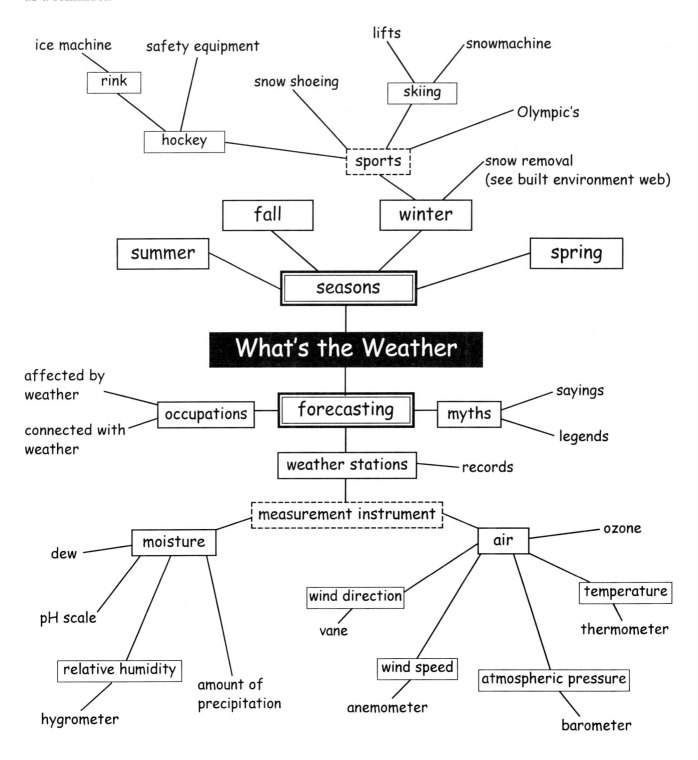

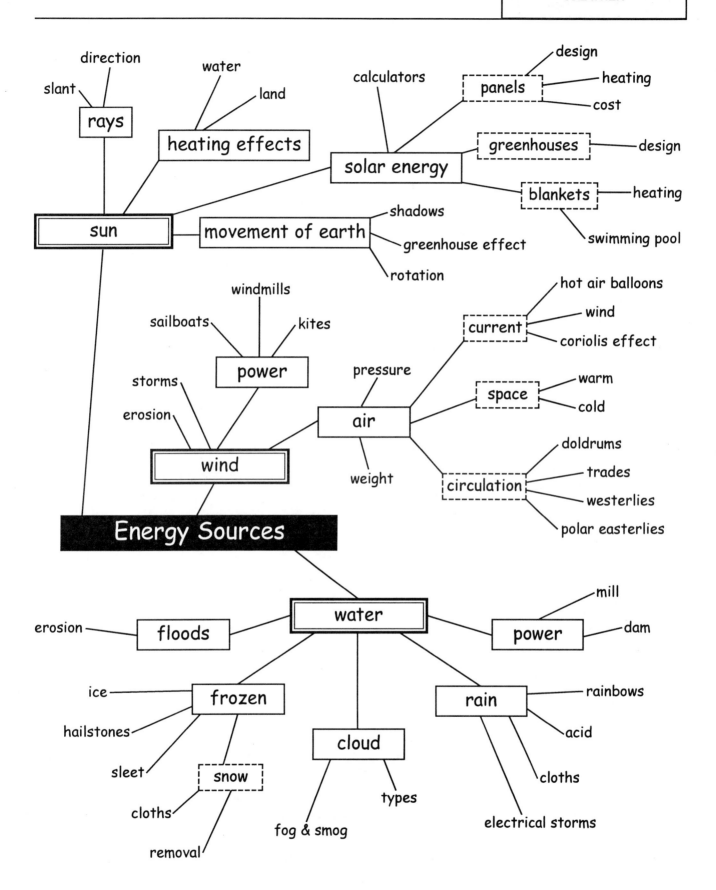

Synopsis

Situation: Campers are transporting their belongings from shore to a campsite.

Problem: Need a device using wind to help transport the load.

Investigation: Use of wind power; friction; other power sources.

Construction: Drawings and scale model.

Evaluation: Compare devices over a course, using fan as wind source.

Helping Hand

Use the web, "Energy Sources" page 83.

More Activity Ideas

Floating Barge, pg 95

Sail Power, pg 95

Lifting Machine, pg 95

Learning about the Internet, pg 96

Lifting Device, pg 110

Move It, pg 127

Teacher Planning Page for *Helpful Breezes*

Students imagine themselves faced with the problem of using wind power to move a load from shore to a campsite. The load will have to be transported over sand, gravel, and/or soil.

Starting Points

- ○ Consider the use of one or more sand-tables.
- ○ Provide students with opportunities to experiment with pulleys and other systems if you wish them to incorporate these technologies into their designs.

Exploring

- ○ Investigate the use of wind power. Discover how this form of energy might be stored for later use.
- ○ Look at objects that involve hydraulic and pneumatic systems. Talk to the high school technology teacher about possible field trips.
- ○ Look at how windmills are used. How do water wheels work?
- ○ Elevators and escalators are both lifting machines that employ pulleys and counterweights. Investigate how these two systems operate.
- ○ Determine a method of testing to determine the maximum mass that could be carried.
- ○ Incorporate a pulley system into the design.

Extending

- ○ The wind you are using is not always reliable. Try to use the same design with different power sources.
- ○ Write detailed instructions for putting the vehicles together by other students. Test the plans by sending instructions to another group.
- ○ Look at different types of transportation vehicles. Investigate alternate sources of energy, such as elastic bands or springs.
- ○ Experiment with computer controls systems for the vehicle.

Stimulate Further Thinking by Asking:

- ○ What kind of vehicle could transport you to the island and then be used on land as well?
- ○ What modifications would you need to make to be sure it would work?
- ○ If you find that the best design is superior on land than on water, or the other way around, which considerations are the most important?
- ○ What parts would you be willing to compromise?
- ○ How could you make your vehicle more efficient?

Helpful Breezes

You and your friends decide to spend the summer camping in a beautiful wilderness park. You plan on exploring some of the many islands in the area. There are small boats that can get you and your belongings to the islands. But you need to move your belongings from the shore to your campsite once you get to the islands. Fortunately, there is also a steady, strong breeze coming on shore.

Design a device that will move your things from the boat to your campsite. You want to be able to move as much as possible on each trip. Some of the objects will be heavy and hard to carry.

There's got to be a way to make use of all this energy!

Think About It

1. What shapes for the bottom, or bed, of the device would work best over sand and gravel?
2. What mass can actually be put on this bed?
3. How could you find out if your device would be practical in size? That is, how large a load a full-sized device could transport?
4. How will you test your device?
5. How much space will you need to give a good indication of its speed?
6. What kind of notes should you take so that a complete picture is given when presenting the final report? Will drawings be helpful?

Circle your choice for this project.

1. I worked well with others.

<u>Always</u>   <u>Sometimes</u>   <u>Not Often</u>

2. I tried different ideas.

<u>Always</u>   <u>Sometimes</u>   <u>Not Often</u>

3. I did my best.

<u>Always</u>   <u>Sometimes</u>   <u>Not Often</u>

4. I feel this way about my accomplishment:

_____

Synopsis

Situation: Students want to monitor the weather.

Problem: Need a device to measure an aspect of weather.

Investigation: Weather monitoring devices; local conditions; climate around the world.

Construction: Drawings and verbal descriptions up to working models.

Evaluation: If working models are built, evaluate by combining devices into a class weather station outside.

Helping Hand

Use the web, "What's the Weather" page 82.

View live satellite images of the weather on the Internet.

More Activity Ideas

The Daily News, pg 79

The Lunar Shelter, pg 79

Quick Shelter, pg 94

Learning about Weather Satellites, pg 96

Equilateral Shapes, pg 126

Whirligig, pg 127

Teacher Planning Page for *Weather Watch*

Design and build a device that will measure one element of weather that you are concerned about. Since the device will be exposed to all kinds of weather conditions, it must be very durable.

Starting Points

- ○ What outdoor space can be used for testing weather instruments for both short and long periods of time?
- ○ What other samples of satellite technology can be examined by students to assist them in their understanding of communication technology?
- ○ What trips can be taken to give students a better idea of island conditions and weather reporting?
- ○ How will the results be recorded?

Exploring

- ○ List devices that could be used to record various elements of weather.
- ○ Contact local environmental services and agencies for additional resources.
- ○ Record daily temperature and rainfall for the school area. Chart the results. Employ a graphing software program.
- ○ Use newspapers to find and record weather data for the local area as well as other parts of the world. Examine weather charts for surrounding areas. Mark these locations on a large wall map. Keep a daily record.
- ○ Search for information on weather on Internet. Compare the weather data found on this resource with that in the newspaper, radio, and television.
- ○ Select one location for further study. Make predictions for weather conditions for that area. Check accuracy the next day and chart results.

Extending

- ○ Design and construct a total weather station with members of the class.
- ○ Construct a model of the weather station site on the island.
- ○ Investigate the use of satellites by meteorologists. Download images taken from weather satellites and use these in the class study.

Stimulate Further Thinking by Asking:

- ○ What kinds of weather conditions might affect living on this island?
- ○ What weather conditions are reported for the school area?
- ○ What period of time should be considered when these conditions are being recorded?

Weather Watch

What is the weather like outside?

Find out for yourself.

Build something to help you watch the weather without going outside!

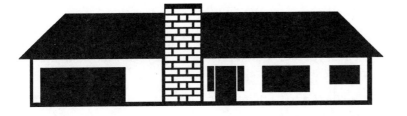

Synopsis

Situation: A natural disaster has struck a town.

Problem: To provide emergency shelter for a night from rain and wind.

Investigation: Storms; local conditions; climate around the world; emergency response; living outdoors.

Construction: Drawings and written descriptions up to scale model.

Evaluation: Safety and ability to keep out water and wind are prime considerations. Models could be tested for waterproofing using a hand-held water sprayer.

Helping Hand

Use the webs, "What's the Weather" and "Energy Sources" on pages 82-3.

View live satellite images of the weather on the Internet.

More Activity Ideas

Finding the Strongest Structure, pg 78

The Lunar Shelter, pg 79

The Daily News, pg 79

Cubes, pg 94

Quick Shelter, pg 94

Equilateral Shapes, pg 126

Teacher Planning Page for *After the Storm*

Following a natural disaster, such as a tornado or hurricane, many residents must cope by making their own emergency shelter out of found materials. **Note**: If you are concerned that some students will be feeling anxious about this scenario, change it to a need for a quick shelter from the rain during a sports tournament.

Starting Points

❍ Many children are afraid of weather conditions they do not understand. What information will be necessary to allay these fears?

❍ What resources might you use to give a good picture of the weather conditions of interest to the students?

Exploring

❍ Find out how the process of naming hurricanes was started. Make a list of names used for hurricanes and track their history.

❍ Investigate the differences between hurricanes, tropical storms, tornadoes and monsoons. Mark the locations of these phenomena on a world map. Keep a record of these weather related activities over a period of time. Discover how weather satellites are used in tracking hurricanes.

❍ Look at forms of emergency shelters. Contact local emergency agencies such as the Red Cross to learn about their role.

❍ Examine shelters that would be common (tents, etc.) and discover why they are efficient protection from the elements.

Extending

❍ You live in a high-risk area and must have alternative shelter available. Construct your alternate shelter so that it can be moved around.

❍ Another family needs shelter and you decide to enlarge your shelter to fit them in.

❍ Talk to "keypals" around the world and find out about their individual weather patterns.

Stimulate Further Thinking by Asking:

❍ How long could you stay in your shelter?

❍ How many additional people can your shelter accommodate?

❍ What changes and additions can you make to your shelter to make life more comfortable during this time?

❍ What other basic equipment can you design that would help to keep you comfortable?

After the Storm

Your community has just be hit by a terrible storm. Although the worst is over and no one has been seriously hurt, most buildings have been damaged. You hear this announcement over the radio.

ATTENTION

All residents of Anytown.

The immediate danger from the storm has passed. The remaining rain and wind will end tomorrow. However many people have been left without shelter. Emergency Aid groups are hurrying to help, but it will take at least 24 hours to provide shelter for everyone.

If possible, please arrange a safe shelter for yourselves until other arrangements can be made. You will find clean drinking water, food, and sanitary facilities at your nearest school. Anyone needing medical attention should be taken to Anytown Hospital.

We repeat, please find shelter for yourselves for the night if you can. Local emergency shelters are already crowded.

**Keep tuned to this station
for further information.**

Think About It

1. What conditions will you need to consider when designing this structure?
2. Make a list of the materials you might be able to find around a home that could be used to make an emergency shelter. How will you represent these materials in your model? (For example, thread could represent rope.)
3. What consideration will you give to eating, sleeping, sanitation, and safety?
4. How will your shelter design include lighting, heating, and ventilation?

Circle your choice for this project.

1. I worked well with others.

<u>Always</u>   <u>Sometimes</u>   <u>Not Often</u>

2. I tried different ideas.

<u>Always</u>   <u>Sometimes</u>   <u>Not Often</u>

3. I did my best.

<u>Always</u>   <u>Sometimes</u>   <u>Not Often</u>

4. I feel this way about my accomplishment:

_____

Synopsis

Situation: Your school is planning a winter play day.

Problem: Need a new event or game.

Investigation: Winter Olympics; winter sports; games; climate.

Construction: Drawings and written presentation followed by a full-sized working prototype.

Evaluation: Game or event must be safe, fun, and accessible to any student who would like to try.

Helping Hand

Use the web, "What's the Weather" page 82.

Have students search the Internet for information on the Olympics.

More Activity Ideas

Teacher Planning Page for *Winter Games*

Students who live in areas where snow and cold weather are part of winter know it can be a great time to play outdoors. The school is planning a winter games day for this year. Students are to come up with designs for a new sporting event or activity that will be fun for all.

Starting Points

○ Think about ways to involve the entire school. For example, events could be designed by groups of older and younger students.

○ Decide when to start this activity in order to provide the time needed during the appropriate weather.

○ Some students will design games that require snow. Schedule an alternative day to try these games in the case of little or no snow.

○ What kinds of activities are featured at a Winter Olympics? Which of these can you adapt?

○ What type of tracks, courses, and/or equipment will be needed?

Exploring

○ Develop plans for an organizing committee. Create roles for each member to make sure that everyone is involved.

○ Your team is submitting the plan to the Olympic Committee as a new sporting event. Prepare a demonstration of your game or event.

○ Research winter sporting activities. Use resources on Internet to find out about the history of the Olympics. Learn about the origins of the events held during the Winter Olympics.

○ Talk to skiers, skaters, etc., and learn about their sport. Invite these individuals into the class.

○ Consider methods for testing tracks and courses.

Extending

○ Adapt the event to work on ground which is frozen but has no snow.

○ Before you are to present your great idea, you find that someone else has designed an event that is very similar to yours. You must be ready to present possible changes to your plan to make both events acceptable.

Stimulate Further Thinking by Asking:

○ Sometimes activities can be combined. How can you do this and what kind of new devices need to be designed for a combined activity?

○ How can the course be changed to make it safe for beginners, for physically challenged people, or for people who need a more challenging course?

Winter Games

SNOW

SLIDE

SLIPPERY

SHIVER

SHOUT

SLIP

SPORT

Winter Games

Synopsis

Situation: A home uses solar energy to produce warmth and electricity.

Problem: Need an additional source of energy to supplement the solar energy.

Investigation: Alternative energy sources, including wind and water; solar energy; construction methods and materials.

Construction: Drawings and written presentation. Could be extended to scale model.

Evaluation: Important criteria include: safety, aesthetics, dependability of source.

Helping Hand

Use the web, "Energy Sources" page 83.

More Activity Ideas

Teacher Planning Page for *Energize!*

A home has been constructed to use solar energy, but this energy is not adequate for the needs of the household. Students are to investigate the possibility of harnessing either wind or water near the house as a supplementary source of energy.

Starting Points

○ You may wish to begin this activity by eliciting students' knowledge about alternative energy sources, then engaging them in a collaborative research activity to gather and share new information.

○ Students need access to water and a drain in order to test water-based models. A water table can be a convenient alternative to a sink.

Exploring

○ Find out about solar homes, including modifications that help provide a constant energy source no matter what the weather conditions.

○ Use the Internet to find and correspond with engineering mentors. Fax preliminary student designs for suggestions.

○ Ask members of the building trades to come to the class to talk about the different aspects of construction (professional associations e.g., the Professional Engineers' Association, parents, relatives, architects).

○ Research different forms of energy and learn about the apparatus that uses these energy sources.

Extending

○ You need a back-up system in case of a power failure to your energy system. How can you extend your system to provide for this possibility?

○ You want to extend the shelter to include a greenhouse to grow your own food. How can you adapt the system to give the needed conditions?

○ Create a budget for the project and devise the systems according to available money and resources. Create a timeline for the completion of the project listing all the jobs to be done and cost/ task.

○ Work with the math teacher on budgeting, interest, loans, etc. Students negotiate loans based on proposals for paying back the money.

Stimulate Further Thinking by Asking:

○ You have a device that seems to work when the energy source is plentiful. What happens when you change the source, e.g. add heat?

○ There is water at the bottom of your hill. How can you transport the water to where you need it?

○ What kinds of devices will you need to make your energy system as efficient as it can be?

Energize!

You have built a wonderful new home on the side of a hill. Generally, solar energy (from the sun's rays) heats the house and supplies the energy to run all the appliances. Unfortunately, it has not been a very sunny year. You find that you will need an additional form of energy to provide warmth and power for appliances.

You have a good supply of both water and wind available close to the house. Design an extra energy system for your house using one element of weather.

Think About It

1. What natural elements provide a form of energy?
2. How are these elements usually harnessed in order to use them?
3. Where could we see some of these kinds of energy being used?
4. What kinds of illustrations will be most useful for further investigations?
5. How well does your design fit into the appearance of the house and surrounding area?
6. How can you test your device to give a true picture of its usefulness?
7. What kinds of adjustments might be needed for the device?
8. How much planning can be done on the computer?
10. How will this help with the total plan?

Circle your choice for this project.
1. I worked well with others.
Always   Sometimes   Not Often
2. I tried different ideas.
Always   Sometimes   Not Often
3. I did my best.
Always   Sometimes   Not Often
4. I feel this way about my accomplishment:
_____

More Activity Ideas

Quick Shelter

Recommended Materials: 10-15 plastic straws, 20-25 straight pins, 2-3 sheets of newspaper

Late last night, a hurricane hit your community. It left many people without homes. It is very warm right now, but people need a place to stay until more help arrives. Make a model of a quick-to-assemble home suitable for use in this disaster area. Lightweight material is suitable.

- ❍ How can you fold/bend the paper to give the structure more strength?
- ❍ How can pins be used to join the material?
- ❍ What can you do to make the newspaper stronger?
- ❍ How can you adjust the model to accommodate more people?
- ❍ What other materials will be suitable for this shelter?

Cubes

Recommended Materials: several sheets of thin card (experiment with different sizes of card), masking tape or quick-drying glue (stress the wise use of resources), electric fan or hair dryer for testing the cube structures

You are about to renovate your old garage. You would like to experiment with different types of building blocks to find out which ones are strong enough to withstand strong winds. Using one sheet of card, make a closed cube that is as large as possible. (This activity is an excellent beginning activity for students who will later design buildings, villages and towns for a theme. These cubes can be the start of the buildings.) Using these cube-shaped bricks, build a wall that can withstand as great a force as possible.

- ❍ How can you make the largest cube with the least amount of cutting?
- ❍ In what other ways can bricks be stacked to give more strength to walls?
- ❍ How can you fold the card to increase the strength of the brick?
- ❍ How do these cube-shaped bricks compare with the geometric nets developed in math activities?

Milk Shake Delight

Recommended Materials: 1 sheet thin card, marbles, plastic cups, wire, glue, paper clips, scissors

A revolutionary new milk shake is available for children to take to school. The only problem is that it has to be shaken several times before it can be poured from the cup. Devise a system to transfer the ingredients from one cup to another several times to mix up the shake. Make a structure that will transfer marbles from one plane to another three times, thus mixing up the shake.

- ❍ Which materials were required and which were not?
- ❍ How does using the marbles affect the length of time the liquid is in motion?
- ❍ How can you bend the paper clips to get greater movement of the liquid?

Jack and Jill

Recommended Materials: paper tubes, yogurt containers, string, thin card or newspaper

You and your brother Jack are getting tired of climbing that silly hill to get one single bucket of water! You want to enjoy your childhood. There must be a way to transport the water down the hill safely without losing any of it. Design and construct a device that allows you to bring water down the hill with little energy on your part. The device must be light, yet strong.

- ❍ How can you ensure that the water will not spill?
- ❍ How can the device be motorized?
- ❍ How can the device be protected from changes in the weather?

Windballs

Recommended Materials: newspaper, kleenex, tissue paper, electric fan or hair dryer

You helped your father clean the family room last night. You noticed many pieces of fluff under the couch that moved very quickly when a breeze blew by. You were fascinated by the shape of these dustballs. Design a "windball" that demonstrates the principles of air movement and direction. It must be able to roll along the ground when wind acts upon it.

- ❍ What happens to a shape with no sharp edges?

- What happens when you try experiment with windballs using different materials?
- What happens if the wind comes from two opposite directions at the same time?

Rocket Power

Recommended Materials: model glider, straight pins or thumb tacks, elastic bands, heavy card, plastic straws (2 different sizes), tape, thin dowel

The Space Agency has commissioned your team to design a low-cost launching system for their next space project. They want to send up a satellite without using expensive rocket fuel. Design a model launching system for projecting satellites into space. Safety factors must be included.

- Which materials were most efficient in producing the energy needed for projecting an object?
- What is the highest distance of projection?
- How can the device be used repeatedly?
- What safety features did you include?

Lifting Machine

Recommended Materials: thick card, thin elastic, paper fasteners, wire, plastic straw, rubber pad, thread, tape, pin or nail hinge, wooden stick

Construct a device that will allow you to lift an object from the floor to a table.

Floating Barge

Recommended Materials: plastic bottle, aluminum foil, heavy card, plasticine, water table, craft knife

Construct a barge that will carry as great a mass as possible. It must be able to move in a straight line in the harbour.

Paddle Boats

Recommended Materials: plastic bottles, card, elastic bands, paper clips, small pieces of plastic

The new amusement park in the community is going to add paddle boats to the pond. They have set up a design contest to determine which model would be the safest and easiest to operate for everyone, including young children and older individuals. Design and construct your entry for this contest

Full of Hot Air

Recommended Materials: plastic bottles, balloon, length of plastic tubing, plasticine

Construct a boat that will travel as far as possible using air as a power source. Determine how far it will travel.

A Rudder Boat

Recommended Materials: material for making a boat, thin pieces of dowel, balsa wood, glue, craft knife

Design a boat that will move in a straight line all the time by the addition of a rudder.

Sail Power

Recommended Materials: any

You are the skipper of a world-class racing yacht. You commission a designer to devise the fastest sail boat possible. This is the day of the big test. Construct and test various model sail boats to see which one is the fastest. (Hint: Consider shape of sail, angle of sail, types of wind movement, etc.)

YOUR NOTES

Learning about Weather Satellites

Research how satellites transmit data. Explore the difference between geostationary and geosynchronous satellites. Find out about satellites used to transmit weather information. Look at how Landsat images are used to determine environmental problems.

Visual images are reconstructed from numerical codes. Here is an activity students can try:

○ Make an enlarged copy of a photograph from a newspaper and explain the term pixel (smallest picture elements). Discuss how the picture is actually made up of individual pixels to create the larger image.

○ Provide graph paper and coloured pencils to each pair of students. One student acts as the satellite and the second student records the transmitted data on graph paper. The "satellite" creates a simple picture on the graph paper covering an area of approximately 15 cm by 15 cm.

○ The recorder is equipped with three coloured pencils. As the "satellite" sweeps across the page, information is passed on regarding each square on the graph paper. If the square has no image, it is "0" and nothing is shaded in that square. When the square is a light colour, it is shaded with colour "1", mid-colour is "2" and the darkest colour is shaded with colour "3". Each line is therefore made up of a series of different pixels that together make up the picture.

○ Continue until the satellite has made the complete image. (Landsat satellites use this process to send images to Earth.)

○ Repeat the above exercise reversing student roles. Note the differences.

Learning about the Internet

Connect with "keypals" using email services. Conduct studies related to weather conditions. Record the information on a database program.

There are useful Internet addresses for you and your students on page 163 of the Appendix.

YOUR NOTES

HUMAN ACHIEVEMENT

Overview of Activities

Activity	Recommended for Grades*	Project	Recommended Materials	Advance Preparation
Help a Friend	4-6	Design a device to help someone eat while in casts limiting motion.	Found materials, wood, construction kits	Schedule research time in the library or using computer search. *Optional*: invite a health care professional to speak to the class.
Student Artists	K-3	Design a safe platform to use while painting.	Found materials; wood; construction kits	*Optional*: arrange a field trip to examine structures in the community.
New Stadium, Please	4-6	Design a stadium for sporting events.	Cardboard; wood; construction kits; *Optional*: Computer drawing software	Schedule research time in the library or using computer search. *Optional*: supply photographs or videos of stadiums.
Shipwrecked	4-6	Design a vehicle to transport equipment to site.	Found materials suitable for wheels and axles; *Optional*: motors and controls	*Optional*: build a model of the terrain first that can be used to test cars.
Phone Travel	4-6	Design a device to support a cellular phone in a car.	Cardboard tubes and other found materials; velcro strips; fabric	*Optional*: provide toy or model phones to help students with size and shape.

*This recommendation is based solely on the reading level of the student worksheets provided for each activity. Any of these activities could be used successfully with students from K-6 with appropriate presentation and support.

What is the technology in...

Here are sample webs related to the topic of human achievement to help you get started. There are many possible entries and links which could be made. The first sample web explores human society and inventiveness. The second web goes into greater detail about specific human areas of achievement, namely sports and art.

With your students, develop webs like these to generate and record ideas. Post the web(s) in the class as a reminder.

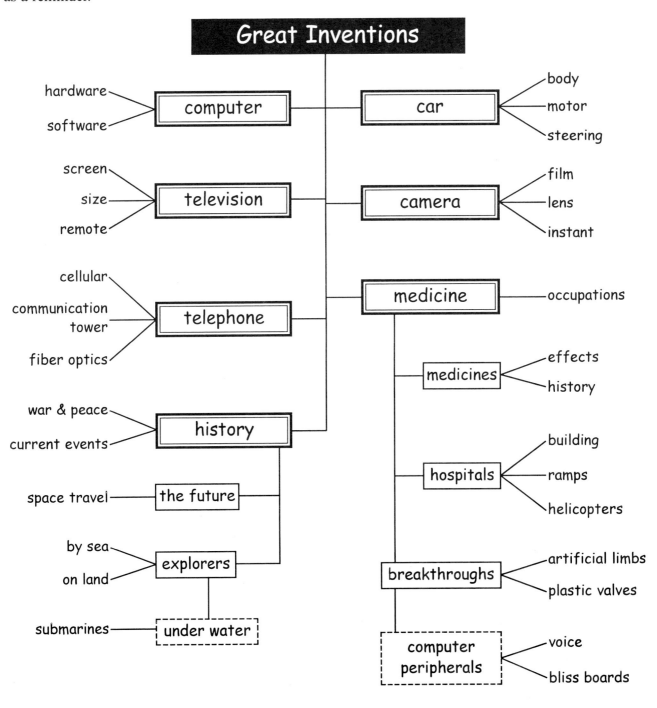

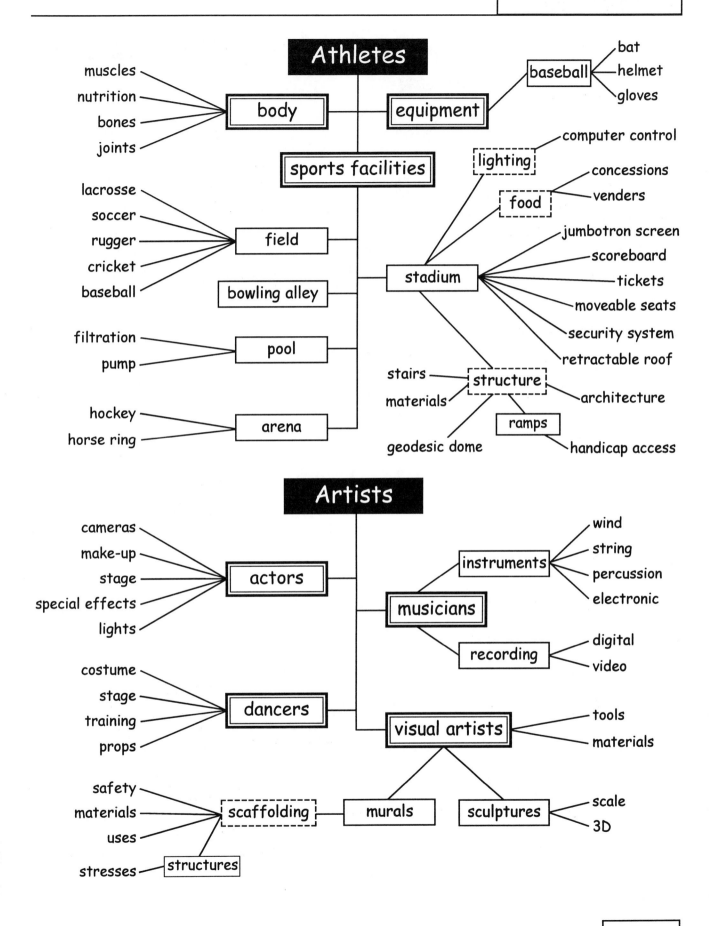

Athletes

muscles
nutrition
bones
joints
→ body — equipment — baseball
- bat
- helmet
- gloves

sports facilities

lighting — computer control

food
- concessions
- venders

lacrosse
soccer
rugger
cricket
baseball
→ field

bowling alley

stadium
- jumbotron screen
- scoreboard
- tickets
- moveable seats
- security system
- retractable roof

filtration
pump
→ pool

hockey
horse ring
→ arena

stairs
materials
→ structure
- architecture

geodesic dome

ramps — handicap access

Artists

cameras
make-up
stage
special effects
lights
→ actors

musicians — instruments
- wind
- string
- percussion
- electronic

recording
- digital
- video

costume
stage
training
props
→ dancers

visual artists
- tools
- materials

safety
materials
uses
→ scaffolding — murals

sculptures
- scale
- 3D

stresses — structures

Synopsis

Situation: A friend has both arms in a cast.

Problem: Need a device to help reach food and drink.

Investigation: Pulleys and levers; assisting devices; care of broken limbs.

Construction: Drawn and written presentation, extend to working model.

Evaluation: Models should be able to reliably lift a piece of plasticine (food) from a table to where a person's mouth would be.

Helping Hand

Use the web, "Human Accomplishments" page 98.

More Activity Ideas

Drawbridge, pg 79

Flagpole, pg 80

Lifting Machine, pg 95

Super Structures, pg 110

Observation Tower, pg 110

Siege Tower, pg 111

Move It, pg 127

Teacher Planning Page for *Help a Friend*

A friend has both arms in casts due to an accident. The casts must remain on for several weeks. The friend is managing pretty well, but finds it difficult to eat and drink without help.

Starting Points

- How could the computer be used to control the device?
- What directional movements must students consider in designing and building this device?
- When should students be sketching their device - during the planning stages or after the device has been tested?

Exploring

- Investigate pulley systems using a variety of materials.
- Look at how levers work and compare levers to the human arm.
- Invite a doctor, nurse or public health speaker to the class to discuss how broken bones are set.

Extending

- Your friend needs to drink plenty of fluids. Make sure that the device can handle both solid food and liquids.
- The patient can sit at a regular table to eat. Design a device that does not interfere with other eaters at the table.
- The patient must stay in bed for 3 weeks. Design a device that could be used to serve meals in bed.
- Your friend and family are going to the park for a picnic. Your device will be used while at the park. Design the device to accommodate its use outside.

Stimulate Further Thinking by Asking:

- Since your friend can only move the casts up and down, how will your device design be affected?
- What type of support will the device need to be free-standing?
- Which materials are most suited to the design?
- What happens to your device when it's not being used?
- How is the device controlled?
- Is there an external control or can the patient manipulate it alone?

Help a Friend

Your friend returns from vacation with both arms in a cast due to an accident. The casts must stay on for several weeks. The casts will only allow up-and-down movement. What really bothers your friend is how difficult it is to eat without help.

You decide to make a device to help your friend.

Think About It

1. How will the plaster casts restrict your friend's movements?
2. What size of device is needed?
3. How can the group work together on this problem?
4. What work can be done on the computer?
5. How can each step of the plan be remembered so that a complete presentation can be given?

Circle your choice for this project.

1. I worked well with others.

Always   Sometimes   Not Often

2. I tried different ideas.

Always   Sometimes   Not Often

3. I did my best.

Always   Sometimes   Not Often

4. I feel this way about my accomplishment:

_____

Synopsis

Situation: Murals will be painted to improve the school's appearance.

Problem: Need a device to help smaller students reach the mural.

Investigation: Construction materials, height and load; structures; materials.

Construction: Drawings and verbal presentation should precede building testable models.

Evaluation: Students should help design a test of the devices using a standard load.

Helping Hand

Use the web, "Artists and Athletes" page 99.

More Activity Ideas

Finding the Strongest Structure, pg 78

Flagpole, pg 80

Cubes, pg 94

Super Structures, pg 110

Teacher Planning Page for *Student Artists*

The parents, teachers, students, and School Board wanted to improve the appearance of your school. The decision is reached to decorate the outside walls of the school with murals painted by students. Since many students are too small to reach the area to be painted, a device is needed for them to be supported safely as they work.

Starting Points

- What field trips might be taken to help give students a better idea of the structures required?
- What information will students need regarding the height versus load capabilities?
- Should the devices be prototype designs or scale models?
- What will the students learn from solving this problem?

Exploring

- Invite painters and interior designers to the class to talk to you.
- Visit construction sites to explore various methods employed by professionals for reaching high places.
- Use a variety of construction kits to make models.
- Work with materials such as straws and cardboard to determine possible solutions.

Extending

- The school is located at the top of a hill. The safety device must have features that will lock it in place when it is placed on a slope.
- The student artists need containers for the paint. They cannot hold the containers while they are painting.
- All equipment must be stored at night and on weekends. Include this consideration in the plans.
- What features can be built into the design so that paint doesn't splatter on people standing on the ground?

Stimulate Further Thinking by Asking:

- How could natural environment of the school be included in the design?
- How will your design be moved to another section of wall space?
- What would be the best size for this device?

Student Artists

What is the artist painting?

Synopsis

Situation: Community is ready to build a new stadium.

Problem: Need a design for the stadium.

Investigation: Construction techniques and materials; sports; access; structures.

Construction: Drawings, written and verbal presentation, scale model.

Evaluation: Have students act out a town meeting in which all of the proposals are considered.

Helping Hand

Use the web, "Artists and Athletes" page 99.

Use the Internet to view different stadium designs.

More Activity Ideas

Stable Platform, pg 78

Learning about the Internet, pg 96

Observation Tower, pg 110

Geodesic Dome, pg 126

Playground Amusement, pg 126

Teacher Planning Page for *New Stadium, Please*

A community is planning to build a stadium. Proposals are being requested from local contractors and designers. The proposals must consist of a scale model, written, and verbal presentation.

Starting Points

○ Encourage students to research stadium designs.

○ Decide if each group will work on separate designs or work on a particular stadium feature for a collaborative class model.

○ How can the computer assist in the planning of the stadium models?

Exploring

○ Work on creating different structures using a variety of materials and shapes.

○ Determine why the architecture of domed stadiums, such as Toronto's SkyDome, makes them very sturdy structures.

○ Explore objects in the natural world for possible links (spider webs, etc.)

Extending

○ The stadium needs 3 seating levels to allow a clear view of the play area.

○ The stadium will be used all year round. How can you make sure the spectators will be protected from inclement weather?

○ The stadium must be accessible to physically challenged people.

○ The stadium will sometimes be divided for two smaller events taking place at the same time. consider a way to section off the stadium.

Stimulate Further Thinking by Asking:

○ Where will physically challenged visitors be seated? How will they reach their seats?

○ How will large numbers of people enter and exit the stadium?

○ What services and facilities are needed to make visitors comfortable?

New Stadium, Please

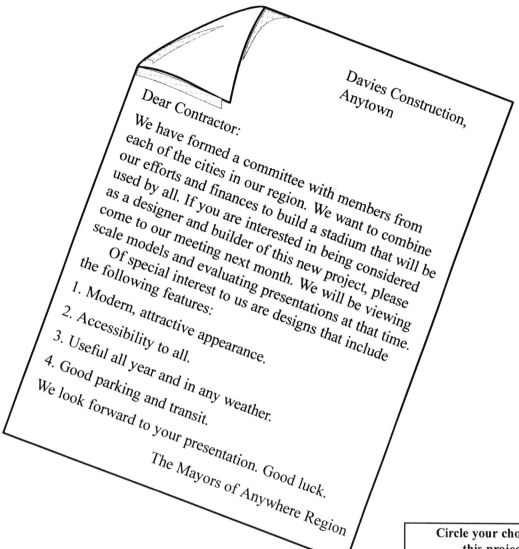

Davies Construction, Anytown

Dear Contractor:

We have formed a committee with members from each of the cities in our region. We want to combine our efforts and finances to build a stadium that will be used by all. If you are interested in being considered as a designer and builder of this new project, please come to our meeting next month. We will be viewing scale models and evaluating presentations at that time. Of special interest to us are designs that include the following features:

1. Modern, attractive appearance.
2. Accessibility to all.
3. Useful all year and in any weather.
4. Good parking and transit.

We look forward to your presentation. Good luck.

The Mayors of Anywhere Region

Think About It

1. What is needed in your stadium design to sell it to the mayors' committee?
2. How will you show the committee that your design is the best for all purposes?
3. Which construction materials will work best for the plan?
4. What shape will be best for the building?
5. What materials will be the best for the prototype?
6. How many times will the design be revised?

Circle your choice for this project.

1. I worked well with others.

Always   Sometimes   Not Often

2. I tried different ideas.

Always   Sometimes   Not Often

3. I did my best.

Always   Sometimes   Not Often

4. I feel this way about my accomplishment:

_____

Synopsis

Situation: Ocean explorers have a base camp in a hard-to-reach location.

Problem: Need a way to transport delicate equipment to the camp (overland).

Investigation: Ocean exploration; transportation; wheels and axles; control devices.

Construction: Drawings, written and verbal presentation, followed by a testable scale model.

Evaluation: Models should be tested over various surfaces.

Helping Hand

Use the web, "Human Accomplishments" page 98.

Search the Internet using these terms: sunken treasure, sunken ships, ocean exploration.

More Activity Ideas

Teacher Planning Page for *Shipwrecked*

A transportation crew must design a vehicle that can transport fragile equipment over rocky, seaside terrain in support of an expedition hunting sunken ships.

Starting Points

- ❍ How will they learn about wheels and axles which will help them in this activity?
- ❍ How can computer control devices be included in this activity?
- ❍ How can the vehicles be tested and evaluated?

Exploring

- ❍ Research activities carried out by ocean explorers.
- ❍ Work with different vehicle designs to determine the best shape and construction techniques.
- ❍ Test the vehicles in sand- and water-tables to determine what mass the vehicles can carry.

Extending

- ❍ Cargo in the wreck must be raised to the surface without loss. Devise a method of raising the cargo from the sea floor.
- ❍ Very sensitive electronic instruments are used to locate shipwrecks. How will you store this equipment safely?
- ❍ Construct a model of the sunken ship.

Stimulate Further Thinking by Asking:

- ❍ What are the dangers of searching underwater?
- ❍ What factors will affect the raising of cargo from deep water?
- ❍ What kinds of treasures from the past may be found?
- ❍ How would learning about past explorers help solve this problem?
- ❍ Where will the objects be stored when they are brought to the surface?

Shipwrecked

Over the years, hundreds of ships have been wrecked at sea. In recent times, modern explorers and researchers have begun investigating the wreckage of famous ships such as the Titanic and the Mary Rose. Your group wants to help in these shipwreck investigations.

One problem for the researchers is that the site for the base camp is very hard to get to by regular transportation. It is near the sea and the area is very rocky. Your group is the Transportation Crew and it is your responsibility to deliver all the high-tech equipment to the base camp by the end of the month.

Design and construct a vehicle that will carry all necessary equipment to the site of the expedition. Consider factors such as the weather conditions, the number of people who will have to be transported to the site, and the road conditions.

Think About It

1. Where can information about shipwrecks be found?
2. How will this information help in the plan of the model?
3. What equipment will be needed for the shipwreck investigation?
4. How can the ocean bottom be reached safely?
5. Where are sunken ships found? Which oceans? What part of the world?
6. What can be done if the first vehicle does not work properly?

Circle your choice for this project.

1. I worked well with others.

Always   Sometimes   Not Often

2. I tried different ideas.

Always   Sometimes   Not Often

3. I did my best.

Always   Sometimes   Not Often

4. I feel this way about my accomplishment:

Synopsis

Situation: More people are using car phones.

Problem: Need a way to hold the phone so it can be used while the car is temporarily stopped.

Investigation: Communication devices, car interior design, ergonomics.

Construction: Drawings, written and/or verbal presentation. Could extend to prototype.

Evaluation: User's comfort, security, durability are all important criteria.

Helping Hand

Use the web, "Human Accomplishments" page 98.

More Activity Ideas

Flagpole, pg 80

Super Structures, pg 110

Observation Tower, pg 110

Morse Code, pg 110

Heavy Duty Bag, pg 112

Teacher Planning Page for *Phone Travel*

More and more people are finding cellular phones both convenient and helpful. Unfortunately, using these phones while driving in a car has proven to be a dangerous distraction for the driver. And it is not always easy to find a secure place to put the phone between stops. What kind of device would keep a cellular phone conveniently close at hand in a car?

Starting Points

○ Students should begin by making "mockup" cellular phones from cardboard, wood, or construction kits.

○ What useful background resources such as communication devices, car design, steering systems can be used for this activity?

○ What materials are students likely to request?

○ How can students be encouraged to sketch plans before constructing?

Exploring

○ Investigate devices used by physically challenged individuals to help them in their daily lives.

○ Invite people who do mouth paintings or use Bliss symbol boards for communication to your class to discuss what features are needed in such a design.

Extending

○ Motor vehicles come in many shapes and sizes. Make sure the design will fit any type of vehicle.

○ Passengers in the back seat of a car or in the back of the van may want to use the device. Consider this possibility in the plan.

○ Some phones have a cord which is plugged into the car's cigarette lighter to recharge the phone's battery. How could you modify your device to suit this need?

Stimulate Further Thinking by Asking:

○ Where will the device be kept when not in use?

○ What is the best location for the device?

○ What other uses can be suggested for the device?

Phone Travel

Many people are keeping in touch with home and business as they travel by having a phone in their car. Car phones, sometimes called cellular or mobile phones, are very convenient ways of communicating. But they can be a distraction to drivers. The phones are small enough to fall on the floor or to roll away on the seat. A person stretching to pick up a phone is not able to pay attention to traffic conditions.

Design and construct a device that allows car drivers to use their phones more safely when stopped beside the road or in parking lots.

Owner's Manual for a Cellular Phone

General Safety Information

Safe Rules for Driving

Safe driving is your first priority. Keep your hands on the wheel and your eyes on the road.

Check the laws and regulations on the use of cellular telephones in the areas where you drive. Always obey them. Also, when using your phone in your car, please:

- Give full attention to driving.
- Use hands-free operation if available.
- Pull off the road and park before making or answering a call.

Page 7

Think About It

1. What are the different motor vehicles?
2. Where will the device fit?
3. What materials can you bring from home?
4. Could someone using your device easily take notes?
5. What part of the group presentation can be prepared on the computer?
6. How will the models be tested?

Circle your choice for this project.

1. I worked well with others.

Always   Sometimes   Not Often

2. I tried different ideas.

Always   Sometimes   Not Often

3. I did my best.

Always   Sometimes   Not Often

4. I feel this way about my accomplishment:

_____

More Activity Ideas

Super Structures

Recommended Materials: toothpicks, popsicle sticks, straws, Plasticine (or marshmallows, ju-jubes, etc), small weights

On a visit to construction site, you noticed that the builders use a great many supports while constructing buildings. You wondered how strong these different structures really are. You set up an experiment to test your theories. Build as tall a structure as possible. Try and use the least amount of material yet build the tallest structure.

- How can you test the strength of the structure?
- What is the greatest mass that can be supported with the minimum amount of material?
- Which adhesive materials are the most (least) effective?
- How could you build the structure as wide or as long as possible?

Observation Tower

Recommended Materials: straws, thin card, tape, scissors

Oil has been discovered in Lake Erie. Your engineering company has been commissioned to design and construct an observation tower for the project. The tower will sit on a platform in the middle of the lake. The lake can get very rough and so the tower must be very strong yet flexible. Make a model of this tower that is least 1 m high. The structure should be as stable as possible.

- What is the largest structure you can build?
- Does your design withstand a test in water?
- How can you test the structure for strength and flexibility?

Lifting Device

Recommended Materials: 2 sheets of thin card, thin string, 4-6 paper clips, 1 paper cup, scissors

Your sister's prized model car is at the bottom of a deep hole and it is your responsibility. You were told not to play with it when she wasn't there. You have to get it back before she comes home from school. The house is locked and you can only find a few objects.

Devise a plan to retrieve the car. Design and construct a means of lifting the car vertically without damaging it.

- How many pulleys make the lifting device efficient?
- How do pulleys assist in making it easier to lift the car?
- How does placement affect the lifting device?

Hidden Treasure

Recommended Materials: objects to represent the scientific treasures: coins in a plastic net at bottom of a water tank or water table, deflated balloon, plastic tubing, Ping-Pong balls, thread, elastic bands

Deep below the surface of the water lies a treasure of scientific information. Your job as the leader of the expedition is to discover a method of raising the objects to the surface of the water without physically lifting them up. They must be undamaged for the scientists. Design a device that will be able to bring the objects to the surface of the water. The objects must be undamaged during the lift to the surface.

- What happens if there is air inside the tubing?
- What is the greatest mass raised by this device?
- How can a pulley system make the device more efficient?

Morse Code

Recommended Materials: 2 small cardboard boxes with lids, 2 4.5 V batteries, bulb holders with 3.5 V bulbs, wire, aluminum foil, paper fasteners, card, elastic bands, masking tape, scissors

You and your friends have built a tree house that is reached by climbing a ladder. You want to find a way of communicating with someone at the foot of the ladder without having to lean out and talk.

Castles

Recommended Materials: thin card, masking tape, scissors, string, spools, straight pins, pieces of dowel, lid from a jar

Build a castle or fort for the knights. It must be safe, strong, and capable of being defended easily. Consider adding these features: drawbridge that can be operated manually (or adapted with an electric motor), moat that surrounds the castle, spiral staircase within the tower.

Siege Tower

Recommended Materials: heavy card, lids from cardboard boxes, paper tubes, spools or objects of wheels, straws, paper fasteners, masking tape, glue, scissors, springs, plastic film containers containing marbles

A siege tower was often part of the fortress in medieval times. It was a large, mobile structure that was pushed towards the high curtain wall. Inside, troops has some protection as the structure was covered in wet animal hides. On reaching the battlements, the tower's drawbridge was lowered and battle commenced. Construct a model of a siege tower that is at least 60 cm high, is capable of supporting a 1 kg mass, and has a drawbridge that operates by counter-weights.

Battering Rams

Recommended Materials: plastic bottle, cardboard tubes, glue, masking tape, string, wood, dowel, cardboard corners, elastic bands

As castles became more sophisticated, so did the designs of the battering rams used to break down the walls. Construct a battering ram that can break down the walls or drawbridge of the fortress. It must be able to swing freely back and forth from its frame support.

Catapults

Recommended Materials (only these): wooden sticks, glue, elastic bands, paper (for the rocks), cup hooks, string, small rubber or Ping-Pong balls

Soldiers in medieval times faced many hazards. During battles, forts would be under siege. It might be several days before help would appear. Come up with a device to keep the enemy away from the fort until reinforcements arrive. The wall of the model fort is 2 m high.

Egyptian Times

Recommended Materials: sugar cubes, simple construction kits

In ancient Egyptian times, pharaohs were buried in elaborate tombs inside pyramids. Each pharaoh ordered the construction of the tallest and largest pyramid yet to show the power of his or her empire. (Or have students investigate how to use pulleys to lift heavy blocks into place to form a pyramid. Supply spools, string, elastic bands, etc.)

Viking Vessel

Recommended Materials: straws, glue, plastic, aluminum foil, other

Construct a model of a Viking vessel. Start with a prototype out of straws and glue, then make another boat from a more substantial material that must float, not tip over, and be able to support a substantial mass.

Medieval Times

Encourage students to conduct research in this area before they do these activities so that they understand the use of simulated materials available for the times, the types of community organization, battles, etc.

Heavy Duty Bag

Recommended Materials: one sheet of paper, glue, dried beans (to test the bag)

Design and make a closed paper bag to carry as much mass as possible. The bag must not burst when dropped from a height of 1 m. (Or design a bag to carry as much volume as possible.)

Lighthouse

Recommended Materials: any

Design and make a lighthouse that is as tall as possible and with a flashing light on the top. (The light must go on and off in order to warn ships of dangerous rocks nearby.)

Jewel Thief

Recommended Materials: any

You are responsible for guarding the most precious jewels in the land. Devise a system that will turn a light on to warn you if the jewels are about to be taken from their stand.

YOUR NOTES

BUILT ENVIRONMENTS

Overview of Activities

Activity	Recommended for Grades*	Project	Recommended Materials	Advance Preparation
Keep It Small	4-6	Design a device to reduce waste volume.	Found materials; construction kits; reusable containers; 3-D Geometric shapes	*Optional*:Combine with a science/math activity on volume. *Optional*: supply catalogues from hardware stores.
A New Street	K-3	Design all the elements for a new street.	Found materials; plasticine; sand; toy cars, etc.	*Optional*: arrange a class visit with an older/physically challenged person.
Towering Heights	4-6	Design an office tower that allows light to reach its surroundings.	Cardboard; plastic sheets; construction kits; found materials *Optional*: Computer drawing software	Schedule research time in the library or using computer search. *Optional*: arrange to visit an area with office towers.
Play Time	K-3	Design a new play area.	Found materials; construction kits; natural materials.ie. dry grass or sticks	*Optional*: divide into groups that each make one component of play area.
Raise It	4-6	Design a device to transport people up a hill.	Found materials; wood; elastic bands; pulleys; *Optional*: motors and control devices.	*Optional*: decide on testable parameters such as ability to move an object up a 1 m ramp.

*This recommendation is based solely on the reading level of the student worksheets provided for each activity. Any of these activities could be used successfully with students from K-6 with appropriate presentation and support.

What is the technology in...

Here are sample webs related to the topic of built environments to help you get started. There are many possible entries and links which could be made. In the webs on these two pages, the distinction is made between transportation systems and other components of a typical city.

With your students, develop webs like these to generate and record ideas. Post the web(s) in the class as a reminder.

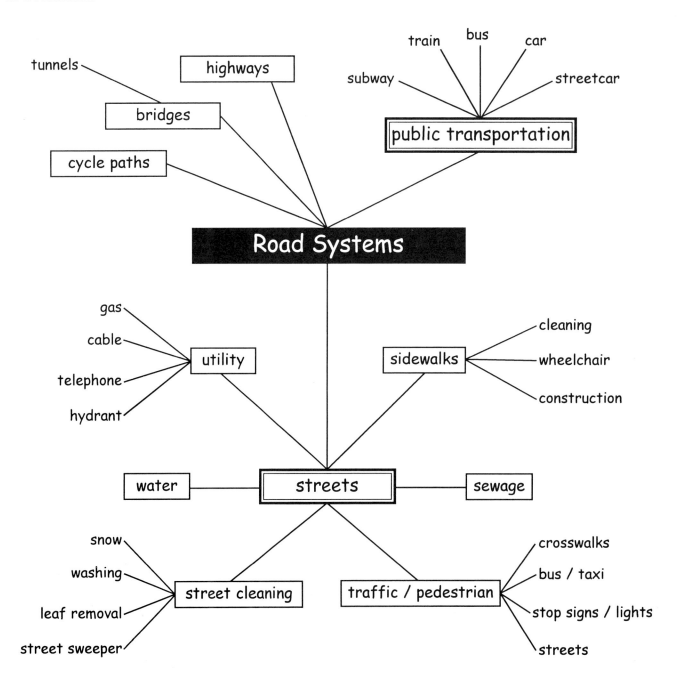

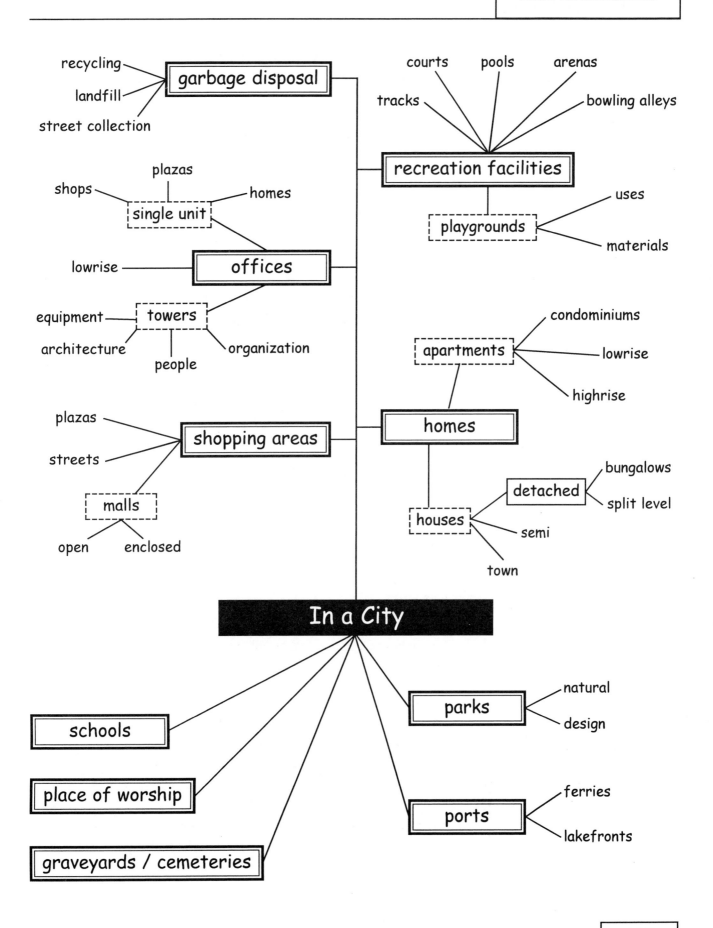

Synopsis

Situation: Contest to see who can reduce waste volume.

Problem: Variety of waste materials to be sorted, compressed, and stored.

Investigation: Recycling; waste management; properties of materials; decomposition.

Construction: Drawings and oral presentation, up to a working prototype.

Evaluation: Devices should be easy to use, sturdy, and succeed in reducing waste volume.

Helping Hand

Use the web, "In a City" page 115.

More Activity Ideas

Finding the Strongest Structure, pg 78

Cubes, pg 94

The Geodesic Dome, pg 126

Teacher Planning Page for *Keep it Small*

A device is needed to help reduce the volume of waste discarded by a family. The device can sort and or compact the waste. Students are to consider cleanliness and convenience as well as function.

Starting Points

- What preplanning activities will be used to focus students on the garbage problem and the need to reduce, recycle, and reuse?
- What field trips will be appropriate?
- Who will be available to speak to the class on the topic?
- How will students be grouped to develop these different machines?
- What construction materials will be suitable for a topic on recycling?
- What materials will be suitable for the devices to accommodate the extra mass of compressed objects?

Exploring

- Look at ways of reducing garbage output.
- Talk to local environmental groups concerned with waste reduction.
- Investigate trash compactors and garbage disposal devices.

Extending

- Design a device that will process leftovers from the lunchroom, grass clippings from the school garden, and other materials.
- Design a composter for the school or home that will be easy to use in the cold winter months when it is harder to get to the unit stored in the backyard.
- Consider methods of separating metal cans from the rest of the garbage.
- Your family subscribes to two daily newspapers. Design a storage system that will contain this amount of newsprint each week.
- Recycling trucks have separate sections for the different materials. Consider ways to help the workers by making sorting easier.

Stimulate Further Thinking by Asking:

- In what ways can your device be made more efficient?
- How can the storage device operate on sources of power other than human?
- What can be modified to make the storage device easier to take to the pickup point on the street?

Keep It Small

There is less money these days for municipal services in your community. As a result, your community has had to cut back on garbage pick-up. Each home is now allowed to put out only one large green garbage bag (biodegradable, of course) per week. Your family is used to putting out two or three large bags of garbage every week.

What methods will reduce the amount of garbage per household?

Design and build a device that will process garbage so the waste material takes up less room. The device will need to be kept in a small cupboard during the week. It will have to be stored all year and consideration needs to be given to storage during warmer weather.

WASTE REDUCTION CONTEST
Join in the effort to cut down
on waste and you can win!

First Prize: A family membership for one year to Anytown's Community Athletic Club. Swim, sauna, exercise, and join in the fun for free!

Other prizes include passes to upcoming concerts and other events at the Anytown Arena.

All you have to do is help the environment.

Here's how it works.

Sign up for the Waste Reduction Contest. The number of bags of garbage your family produces will be counted. Each week your family puts out less than three bags for collection, you'll be entered into the contest.

Think About It

1. What research will be needed before the activity is started?
2. How can the garbage in the class simulate the real problem?
3. What safety considerations are needed for this device?
4. What kind of junk materials can be used for the models?
5. How can the invention be marketed?
6. In what ways can a computer assist in the plan of this device?

Circle your choice for this project.

1. I worked well with others.

Always   Sometimes   Not Often

2. I tried different ideas.

Always   Sometimes   Not Often

3. I did my best.

Always   Sometimes   Not Often

4. I feel this way about my accomplishment:

_____

Synopsis

Situation: A new street is needed.

Problem: Street must accomodate all users, including seniors.

Investigation: Road systems; physical challenges; accessibility; lighting.

Construction: Drawings and oral presentation, up to a scale model by the class.

Evaluation: Consideration to accessibility and safety is important. Will the street, as designed, suit everyone?

Helping Hand

Use the web, "Road Systems" page 114.

Search the Internet for city maps and views of roads.

More Activity Ideas

Drawbridge, pg 79

Lifting Device, pg 110

The Simple Bridge, pg 126

Teacher Planning Page for *A New Street*

District planners want to encourage complete accessibility for all the residents throughout the community but especially on the new street where a senior's home is to be built. Some of the people living in the home will be in wheelchairs or walk with the assistance of a cane or walker. The new street must take into account the senior's needs.

Starting Points

○ Take students on a walk around the school area to examine the structures that make up a street.

○ Invite some senior citizens to visit with students. Students should have questions ready to ask about what the seniors find helpful and difficult about local streets. (The same seniors could be invited to help evaluate the final projects.)

Exploring

○ Examine wheelchairs and determine how steep an incline can be used on the curb.

○ How can bridges be used in the design of the street?

○ Examine plans for other communities to determine what factors need to be considered.

Extending

○ Consideration should be given to the size of sidewalks and curbs. Where should utility poles and hydrants be placed?

○ WheelTrans buses will use the street a great deal. How will this factor be included in the designs?

○ What attention will be given to traffic signals to accommodate older citizens (slowing down the signals, alternate devices for the hard-of-hearing or visually impaired adults)?

○ What changes to the street lighting might need to be included?

Stimulate Further Thinking by Asking:

○ Why are street lights important? How could the street lights be designed to come on automatically when it becomes dark?

○ How will older adults be protected from the traffic?

○ What could be added to the street to help older adults who may want to rest periodically?

A New Street

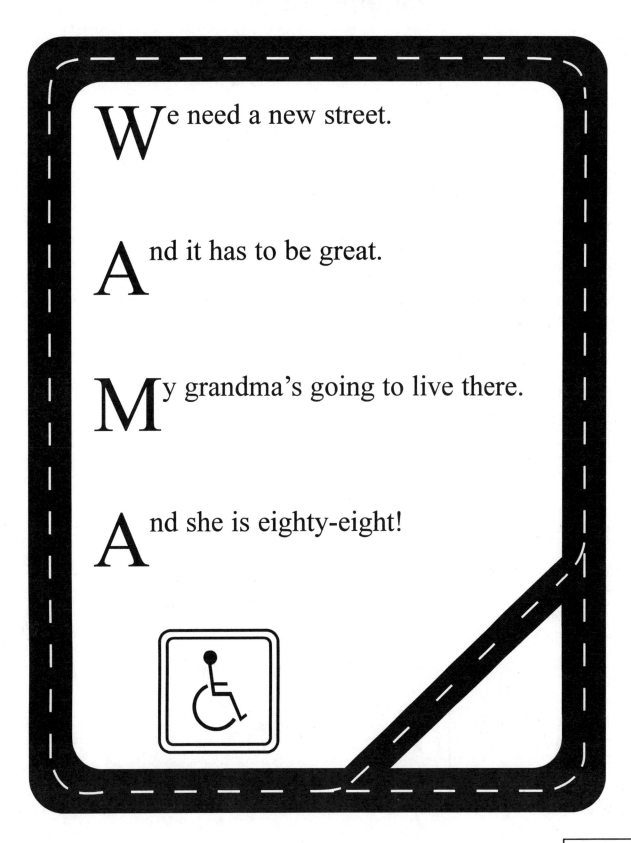

We need a new street.

And it has to be great.

My grandma's going to live there.

And she is eighty-eight!

Synopsis

Situation: New tower being built near school.

Problem: To design the tower so it blends with the style of the school building and allows light to reach the school yard.

Investigation: Construction techniques; solar radiation; architecture.

Construction: Drawings and written presentation, with a scale model of the tower and school if time allows.

Evaluation: How well does the proposed design meet the criteria of blending in style and allowing light to pass?

Helping Hand

Use the web, "In a City" page 115.

More Activity Ideas

Teacher Planning Page for *Towering Heights*

New towers, particularly where they might block the sunlight from existing residential and school areas, pose particular problems for designers. It is often necessary to modify the tower design to suit the architectural styles of surrounding buildings. Students are challenged to find a creative solution to a tower proposed near their school.

Starting Points

○ What materials will be best suited to build the office tower?

○ What materials will be appropriate for this activity considering the restriction of light passage?

○ What will encourage students to consider alternative energy sources for the building?

Exploring

○ Examine building codes and city bylaws to determine what guidelines need to be followed.

○ Experiment with various construction techniques to determine how to build strong structures.

○ Work with different materials to find a suitable one for a prototype of this building.

Extending

○ Consider alternative energy sources.

○ What forms of lighting will be used in the building?

○ Think about ways to keep birds from flying into the windows.

○ How could a computer graphics program assist in the design of the building?

Stimulate Further Thinking by Asking:

○ What different materials will help light enter the tower?

○ How will the shape of the office tower affect the natural light reaching the schoolyard?

○ What safety precautions must be considered when building the tower?

○ How many people will work in the office building?

○ What aesthetic qualities need to be considered?

Towering Heights

An office tower is to be built on land next to your school. The architects are concerned about preserving the natural environment. The aesthetic qualities of the neighbourhood must be maintained. Since this is an older, well-established community, it is important that the office tower blends in with the style of architecture in the area.

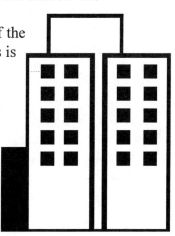

The architects must maximize the space available to them. The building should not cut off the natural light to the schoolyard.

Design and build the office tower to blend with the rest of the area.

Think About It

1. What background information will you need?
2. How can pictures of a variety of office towers be obtained?
3. What modelling material will be suitable for the first prototype?
4. What methods of testing the model tower will be used?
5. How will the models be presented to the class?

Circle your choice for this project.

1. I worked well with others.

Always   Sometimes   Not Often

2. I tried different ideas.

Always   Sometimes   Not Often

3. I did my best.

Always   Sometimes   Not Often

4. I feel this way about my accomplishment:

_____

_____

Synopsis

Situation: Need a new play area for community.

Problem: Area must be fun yet safe, and balance needs of nature with those of users.

Investigation: Play equipment; safety; use of recycled materials.

Construction: Drawings and oral presentation. Extend to models made from construction kits or plasticine.

Evaluation: Creativity should be the primary factor.

Helping Hand

Use the web, "In a City" page 115.

More Activity Ideas

Milk Shake Delight, pg 94

Playground Amusement, pg 126

Whirligig, pg 127

Move It, pg 127

Teacher Planning Page for *Play Time*

A new housing development is to be built in your community. Along with houses, people need parks, playgrounds, and green space. The environment must be protected to ensure a healthy balance between people's needs and the natural beauty of the area. The architects are now planning a community park and playground area.

Safety must be a key concern in the development of the community park and playground area. The area is to be used by people of all ages. They want to use as many recycled or reused materials as possible.

Design a creative area that will satisfy the needs of a variety of age groups. The community park and playground area must be usable all year long.

Starting Points

○ How will students be organized to develop various sections and different equipment for the play area?

○ Where will the playground models be displayed?

○ What pieces of equipment will operate on sources of power other than human?

○ In what way will students record their initial ideas about what the playground will look like?

Exploring

○ What are the features of a creative play area?

○ What are the important safety concerns in a play area?

○ Examine local parks and record who uses them and at what times.

○ Survey the neighbourhood to determine the needs of the community.

Extending

○ Design a section of the play area to be used by young children only.

○ Design a piece of playground equipment that employs a pulley system.

○ Build one section of the playground underground for use on wet days.

○ Devise a section of the play area for parents and others who are watching the young children.

Stimulate Further Thinking by Asking:

○ What unusual piece of equipment can you add to the play area?

○ How can you keep unwanted animals out of the play area?

○ What unusual materials would add interest to the play area?

Play

Time

123

Synopsis

Situation: New mall is being built with parking uphill from the stores.

Problem: How can people be transported to and from the parking lot?

Investigation: Mechanisms; public transit; loads; safety.

Construction: Drawings and written presentation to working prototype of mechanism.

Evaluation: Test the prototypes against a selected standard, such as raising and lowering an object 0.5 m safely.

Helping Hand

Use the web "In a City" page 115.

More
Activity Ideas

Lifting Device, pg 110
Hidden Treasure, pg 110
Siege Tower, pg 111
Move It, pg 127

Teacher Planning Page for *Raise It*

Your community will soon have a new mall, but there is concern about the distance people may have to walk uphill from the stores to the parking lot. A novel and safe means of transporting people and their purchases is needed.

Starting Points

○ What materials will be most suitable for building a working model of the device?

Exploring

○ Work with pulley systems to determine their effectiveness in a variety of situations.

○ Talk to urban planners to find out how this problem of distant access is addressed.

Extending

○ Many visitors to the mall will be parents with young children. Consider how baby carriages and strollers will be transported.

○ Physically challenged shoppers must have full access to the parking area and the mall. How can this be achieved?

○ After shopping, people will have their arms full of packages and be quite tired. Remember, they want a way to get back to their cars with a minimum amount of effort.

Stimulate Further Thinking by Asking:

○ How can the device be designed to carry more passengers?

○ What methods of lighting can be used?

○ How can the device be designed to stop at specific sections of the parking lot?

Raise It

A shopping mall is to be built on a hill near your community. The cars are to be parked in an outside lot at the base of the hill. This area is a good distance from the mall and customers, including many older adults and parents with young children, will have to walk a long distance to get from the parking area to the stores.

You want this mall to appeal to everyone, but you know that the distance between the parking area and the mall will pose a problem. Customers want to shop in comfort. Safety must be a consideration because the mall is open in the evening.

Design and construct a transportation device that will carry people to and from the mall and the parking area. The device must be functional, yet aesthetically appealing.

Think About It

1. Is this a problem that can be worked through alone or would a team be better?
2. How will the device be tested?
3. What safety precautions can be built into the device?
4. How can computer control be used to operate the device?
5. What materials will suit the prototype?
6. How can you use recycled materials in this activity?

Circle your choice for this project.

1. I worked well with others.

Always   Sometimes   Not Often

2. I tried different ideas.

Always   Sometimes   Not Often

3. I did my best.

Always   Sometimes   Not Often

4. I feel this way about my accomplishment:

_____

More Activity Ideas

Equilateral Shapes

Recommended Materials: 2-3 sheets of thin card, hole punch, 1 m of string, 10-15 twist ties, scissors, objects to represent the four people

You and a group of fellow scientists are marooned on a distant planet. Your vehicle had to leave in a hurry and the crew were unable to unload any supplies. It will be several days before your spacecraft returns to rescue your team. You need to prepare a shelter for the evening. You have very little material with which to build this shelter. Four people need to stay inside this shelter. Design and construct a shelter for the evening. It must be large enough for four people.

Questions to stimulate further thinking

○ What shape uses the least amount of material but is still be large enough for four people?

○ How do the twist ties add strength to the model?

○ What methods of folding the cardboard add strength or stability to the model?

The Geodesic Dome

Recommended Materials: several sheets of newspaper, masking tape, straight pins

You were on a class trip to the local park. The climbing apparatus in the park fascinated you. It was very large and strong. You wondered if you could design such a device for the day-care program at the school. Design a piece of playground equipment for young children. Make a prototype of the device. Try to make the structure as strong as possible. Use the geodesic dome structure. (Geodesic means shaped like a section of the earth's surface.)

Questions to stimulate further thinking

○ How can you determine the weight of the dome?

○ Which method is the quickest?

○ What would happen if you tried to construct a geodesic dome using shapes other than triangles?

CN Tower

Recommended Materials: 3 sheets of thin card, alternate: 3-4 sheets of newspaper, tape (limit the amount of tape or the whole roll will be used!)

Your Aunt has sent you a postcard from her vacation to Toronto. The card shows a picture of the CN Tower, the tallest free-standing tower in the world. You decide to make a model of the CN Tower that is as tall as possible using the materials you have. Make it a free standing structure. (Your structure cannot be attached to the table or the floor.)

Questions to stimulate further thinking

○ How can you make a tower that will reach the ceiling?

○ What can you do to keep the tower from falling over?

○ How can you fold the paper or card to make the tallest structure?

The Simple Bridge

Recommended Materials: 3 sheets of thin card, popsicle sticks, masking tape, weights

You are stranded while hiking in the mountains. You come across a deep gully. It is too wide to jump over but you must cross it to get home. Construct a model bridge that will cross a distance of 30 cm. The bridge must be able to support an object that represents the mass of an average person. Use Plasticine or a piece of clay.

Questions to stimulate further thinking

○ What happens if you increase the mass?

○ How can you make the bridge as strong as possible?

○ What happens if you increase the span of the bridge?

Playground Amusement

Recommended Materials: 2 sheets of paper, 2 sheets of thin card, masking tape, scissors, marble

You are the designer of a new playground. The children like to have slides to play on. Design a slide for the park. You would like to take the environment into account when designing this slide. (You can test it with a marble to see if it works.) Make a free standing structure down which a marble can roll. When the marble reaches the end, it must travel as far as possible in the air before landing on the ground.

Questions to stimulate further thinking

O How can you test to see if your design is safe?

O How can a marble show you that the slide works?

O How will the size of the slide affect the speed of the marble in the testing situation?

O What effect will a spiral have on the slide?

Whirligig

Recommended Materials: 1 sheet of paper, 2 straight pins, masking tape, stick or dowel, scissors

There is a new baby in your house! This baby cries a great deal especially at bedtime. You want to keep your baby amused until sleep comes. Design a safe toy that will interest the baby. Make a device that revolves very quickly when you blow on it. Try to make an unusual shape.

Questions to stimulate further thinking

O How does the shape affect the design of your revolving device?

O How does the distance from which you blow on the revolving device affect its speed?

O What features need to be considered with either toy or revolving device to make it safe for a baby?

O If you have joined pieces to make the revolving device, in what ways do they increase the movement of your device?

Move It

Recommended Materials: heavy card, strong elastic bands, popsicle sticks

You are a designer of energy-efficient automobiles. You want to impress your clients with the power of your vehicles. Design a model vehicle whose energy source is elastic bands. It must be light and durable. It must travel as far as possible under its own power.

O What additional materials will be useful in this activity?

O How does the shape of the vehicle affect the

elastic power?

O How do the popsicle sticks contribute to the power of the elastic bands?

Motor Boats

Recommended Materials: small motors, construction kit such as LEGO Dacta

The local authority has decided that power boats will be allowed on the small pond in the park. But these boats must be quiet and attractive. (Hint: think about how you will keep the power packs dry.)

Lifting Mechanism

Recommended Materials: 2 plastic syringes, plastic tubing, card, plasticine, paper, masking tape, weights

Design and construct a means of lifting a mass vertically using a horizontal pressure. (Extension: construct a lifting mechanism that picks objects from a table, moves them 90 degrees, and places them back on the table.)

The Candy Factory

Recommended Materials: any

The candy factory needs a new type of vehicle to carry jelly beans. Hint: Try using a ramp on which the vehicle can leave and enter the factory. Try different forms of energy to move the vehicle

Construction Site

Recommended Materials: any

You are the site manager of a new construction area. Your job is to design machines for use on the site that are clean and safe. You will need to design: cranes, ladders, hoists, cement mixers, and trucks. Construct the necessary equipment for the site.

Traffic Lights

Recommended Materials: any

The mayor of the city has commissioned you to design a series of attractive traffic lights that take into account the different traffic patterns during the day.

Oil Rig

Recommended Materials: any

Make a free standing structure 1m tall that is a s stable as possible. Using any materials you like, equip your structure so that it gives warnings when tilted approximately 5 and 15 degrees from the vertical. Include a final warning sound if the structure is about to fall over completely.

Beef Protection

Recommended Materials: any

Build a free standing structure that will support an bouillon cube as high as possible. The structure must detect any human attempt to remove the cube.

Strong Bridge

Recommended Materials: 5 sheets of paper, masking tape scissors, etc.

Make a structure to span a gap of 2 m between desks. The structure must support as much mass as possible. The bridge may only carry one vehicle at a time, so access must be controlled in some way. Include an alarm sound if the vehicle crossing the bridge has too much mass.

Marble Machine

Make a free standing structure down which a marble can roll. When the marble reaches the end of the structure, it must travel as far as possible in the air before landing on the ground (place a carpet or rubber mat to catch marble). (Control extension: design a device that sorts and counts different sizes of marbles.)

Recommended Materials: 2 sheets of paper, 2 sheets of thin card, masking tape, scissors, marble, etc.

YOUR NOTES

APPENDIX

Contents

Planning Sheets

For Students

Useful Resources

Planning Sheet #1 - Getting Started

Activity _____

Curriculum

General Learning Outcomes

What will students learn from solving the problem posed by this activity? Check the major technological concepts you can develop with students.

Fabrication
- ❏ Structures
- ❏ Materials

Mechanisms
- ❏ Motion
- ❏ Power and Energy
- ❏ Control & Systems

Human Elements
- ❏ Function
- ❏ Aesthetics
- ❏ Ergonomics

_____

_____

_____

_____

Other Outcomes to be Achieved

- ❏ Math
- ❏ Science
- ❏ Language Arts
- ❏ Visual Arts
- ❏ Social Studies (Self & Society, Geography, History)

_____

_____

_____

_____

_____

Student Groupings and Scheduling

- ○ What groupings will be best for this activity?
- ○ How will students be grouped in order to develop a wide variety of approaches and models? (For example, do you wish to allow for initial individual plans and then one collaborative plan?)
- ○ How can students be grouped for maximum co-operation and equal input?
- ○ How much time will be allocated to the project?
- ○ Will you allow students to redesign their products after testing and evaluation?

Recording and Presentation

- ○ What details should be included in the planning sketches?
- ○ When should sketches of the device or product be drawn? (For example, during the planning stages or after the device has been tested?)
- ○ What recording methods will be used for the initial ideas and the final outcome?
- ○ What records will kept for this activity?
- ○ What method(s) of presentation will students use? (Sketch, model, written and/or verbal report)
- ○ What outline will help students with their presentations?
- ○ How will each device be presented to the class as well as other groups?

Student Products

- ○ Should the devices be prototype designs or scale models?
- ○ Will construction kits be used to test ideas or to produce a product? Which kit(s) will you supply?
- ○ Should students produce a three-dimensional model out of clay or other material first?

Evaluation and Assessment

- ○ How can products be tested and evaluated?
- ○ How will the models be tested for safety, usefulness, and aesthetics?
- ○ Will students be performing self- and/or peer-assessment?
- ○ What method of assessment will you use?

Advance Planning

Visits and Field Trips

- ○ Who can visit the class to help students with their plans?
- ○ What field trips can be taken to help students with their initial planning and research?

Displays and Storage

- ○ How much storage and work space will be required?
- ○ How will the available work space affect the size of the device students can produce?
- ○ Where will models be displayed?

Safety

- ○ What safety factors must be considered?
- ○ Are there any new tools or techniques being introduced which require instruction in safe use?
- ○ How will student products be evaluated for safety?

YOUR NOTES

YOUR NOTES

Planning Sheet #2 Resources

Activity _____

Information

- ○ What resources are already available in your classroom and school? Ask the information technologist or librarian in your school to identify resources useful to your class.
- ○ What outside resources are available?
- ○ What human resources can be used?
- ○ What information will students need before the project is started?
- ○ What background information will students need to solve the problem posed by the activity?
- ○ What information will students need to make sure they have considered as many factors as possible in their design?
- ○ Where will students get this background knowledge?
- ○ Could a survey provide useful information for this activity?
- ○ How could students enlist the help of family members in this activity?

Computers

- ○ Where can the computer fit into this activity? Could it be used in research, planning, presentation, and/or as part of the product itself?
- ○ Who could come to the class to demonstrate or teach the use of a computer graphics program?
- ○ How could computer control devices be included in this activity?

Materials

- ○ Which materials will be appropriate to the task?
- ○ Which materials are presently available?
- ○ What reusable or recycled materials could be used?
- ○ Which materials will be most suitable for building a working model of the device or product?
- ○ Which materials could be brought from home for this activity?
- ○ Which materials will need to be collected over a period of time?

Links with Self, School, Community, and Environment

Who can help you? An ongoing list of contacts will be one of the most useful resources you will have.

Contact Name	Date Contacted	Role in the Class	Phone Number/ Address

Copyright © 1996 Trifolium Books Inc.

Planning Sheet #3 Shopping List: Materials

Wondering what might work? You'll find that students will be able to make amazing products out of these and any other simple materials you provide.

Found Material

- ❑ aerosol can caps
- ❑ buttons
- ❑ candles
- ❑ cans
- ❑ cardboard boxes and cartons
- ❑ cardboard cones (from knitting, weaving wool)
- ❑ cardboard pieces, tubes
- ❑ coathangers
- ❑ compact discs and cases
- ❑ computer diskettes
- ❑ cotton reels (thread)
- ❑ egg cartons
- ❑ elastic bands
- ❑ feathers
- ❑ food from the kitchen (tea, sugar, salt, etc.)
- ❑ food trays
- ❑ hair clips
- ❑ ice cream tubs (large freezer type)
- ❑ knitting needles
- ❑ lids (plastic)
- ❑ uncooked pasta pieces
- ❑ marbles
- ❑ margarine tubs
- ❑ fabric scraps
- ❑ milk cartons
- ❑ nails
- ❑ off-cuts of wood
- ❑ old keys
- ❑ paper bags
- ❑ paper clips
- ❑ paper rolls
- ❑ pieces of dowel

- ❑ plastic beads
- ❑ plastic bottles (especially large ones)
- ❑ plastic drink cups and lids
- ❑ plastic film containers (good for glue and paint holders)
- ❑ plastic tubing scraps
- ❑ plastic weights
- ❑ polystyrene packing
- ❑ pop cans
- ❑ popsicle sticks
- ❑ records (45 rpm and LP)
- ❑ samples of paper
- ❑ scraps of aluminum foil
- ❑ seeds
- ❑ shells
- ❑ shoelaces
- ❑ stones and rocks
- ❑ straws
- ❑ string
- ❑ thread
- ❑ wallpaper samples
- ❑ watches (old)
- ❑ wood scraps
- ❑ wool
- ❑ yoghurt containers

Helping Hand

Make sure that if children are collecting this material, they are gathering it from safe places.

More Recommended Materials

- ❑ balsa wood (different sizes)
- ❑ balloons
- ❑ batteries (sealed)
- ❑ battery holders
- ❑ bulb holders
- ❑ bulbs
- ❑ candles
- ❑ coins
- ❑ cones (knitting)
- ❑ dowel (different sizes)
- ❑ electrical wire
- ❑ feathers
- ❑ gears (different sizes)
- ❑ laces
- ❑ liquid detergent
- ❑ magnets
- ❑ magnifying glass
- ❑ pencils
- ❑ plastic pop bottles
- ❑ plastic tubing
- ❑ plastic sheets
- ❑ Plasticine
- ❑ popsicle sticks
- ❑ propellers
- ❑ reinforcing rings
- ❑ rubber tubing
- ❑ scales
- ❑ spools
- ❑ straws (paper, plastic)
- ❑ string
- ❑ supermarket foam trays
- ❑ syringes (different sizes, no needles)
- ❑ timers (stop watch, egg timer)
- ❑ toothbrushes
- ❑ tubes
- ❑ washers
- ❑ weights

- ❑ wheels (different sizes)
- ❑ wire
- ❑ wood (cut to different sizes)

Paper Materials

- ❑ aluminum foil
- ❑ blotting paper
- ❑ cardboard boxes, tubes, etc.
- ❑ cardboard corners (2 sizes)
- ❑ cardboard wheels
- ❑ paper bags
- ❑ sandpaper
- ❑ thick paper, cardboard
- ❑ thin cardboard
- ❑ tracing paper
- ❑ variety of types of paper
- ❑ waxed paper.

Adhesive and Fixing Materials

- ❑ alligator clips
- ❑ bondfast (quick drying)
- ❑ book binding tape
- ❑ cotter pins
- ❑ double sided tape
- ❑ duct tape
- ❑ electrical tape
- ❑ fabric tape
- ❑ hockey tape
- ❑ masking tape
- ❑ nails
- ❑ paper clips
- ❑ paper fasteners
- ❑ pins
- ❑ scotch tape
- ❑ screws
- ❑ thumb tacks

Planning Sheet #4 Shopping List: Tools

Enlist the aid of parents, fellow staff, and community members to built a collection of these basic tools for your students.

- ❑ awl
- ❑ bench hooks
- ❑ chisel
- ❑ compass
- ❑ cutting boards
- ❑ drills, drill bits
- ❑ drill press
- ❑ files
- ❑ glue guns, glue sticks
- ❑ hammers
- ❑ hand held fan
- ❑ hole punch
- ❑ junior cutting knife
- ❑ junior hacksaw (plus extra blades)
- ❑ mitre (miter) box
- ❑ pencil
- ❑ plane
- ❑ ruler
- ❑ pliers
- ❑ rasp
- ❑ rat tail file
- ❑ safety glasses
- ❑ sanding tools
- ❑ scissors
- ❑ screwdrivers
- ❑ spatula
- ❑ spring clamp
- ❑ try square
- ❑ vise
- ❑ wire cutters
- ❑ wire strippers
- ❑ work bench

Planning Sheet #5 Construction Kits (A Review)

As you know, every class and each student will vary in their interest and ability to work with various construction kits. The following comments are provided to help you select the most appropriate kit for your class. (These comments reflect the opinions of the teachers and reviewers involved in preparing the original version of this book only and are not those of the publisher or editor.) Room is provided for your own notes.

Recommended for All Grades

Gear Box

This kits consists of 4 sizes of gears and 3 sizes of axles. A drive gear box that runs from a "C" type battery is included. The pieces can be connected to any one of the base plates or rectangular rod structures included in the kit. The pieces are easy to manipulate.

LEGO

This is a popular construction kit at school and at home. The attitude at home may affect how the kit is used at school. The pieces are bright, colorful, and attractive. Most of the components are durable but some of the pieces like the windows or doors may break if treated roughly. Many replacement parts are available. There are many components available as extras to the basic kit. Bricks are the main component and they clip into each other to form strong structures which can be free standing or placed on base boards. LEGO is very versatile. It can be used with Duplo and LEGO Technic. It is suggested that a large box with many small compartments be used for the pieces rather than the original cardboard box.

Meccano

The traditional Meccano kit is made from metal pieces and includes wheels, nuts and bolts, fastening materials, struts, etc. It is fairly difficult for younger children. There is a new set of Meccano that is made of plastic and is most suitable for younger children. Activity cards are also available.

Ramagon

Ramagon has been used by NASA engineers to create model space stations. It is easy to build with this kit and it works with other construction kits. It is very durable.

Teko

Teko consists of large plastic wheels, gears, and axles that can be used in conjunction with wood pieces, popsicle sticks, yoghurt containers, paper rolls and other "junk" material. Large scale models can thus be created. Motors can also be added.

YOUR NOTES

Zaks

Zaks are brightly colored, plastic triangles that snap together. Although the manufacturers describe the kit as suitable for ages 5 and up, some children may experience difficulty snapping the pieces together. Interesting flexible shapes and designs can be developed with this kit. (Check on availability of this product in your area as it is not uniformly stocked by distributors.)

Recommended for Grade K-3 Students

Big Builder

Big Builder is particularly good for young children because it has brightly colored, large, and durable pieces which are easy for young children to manipulate. It provides instant success for the child. The children can make models that are useful. It can not be used easily with other kits and more than one kit would be required for a small group of children.

Duplo

Duplo consists of baseboards and bricks of the LEGO variety. The pieces are large and easy to use for young children. Supplementary kits are available. These include pieces for trains, interlocking tracks, people, arches and wheels. Duplo is excellent for introducing skills in the use of LEGO construction. It can be used in conjunction with LEGO, but a large quantity of pieces are needed for groups of more than two. It is a good kit to encourage imaginative play.

Lasy (Imaginit)

This kit is made up of large, brightly colored plastic rectangles, connectors, and round pieces. It fits together easily and is very good for young children. It comes in a variety of kits and sizes. Wheels are available in the kits. New kits have gears and can be motorized. This is a very versatile kit. A large table can be purchased that gives children a base for their work. Pieces of the kit fit neatly inside the centre of the table for easy storage.

Matador

This kit is made from solid beech and employs an interlocking peg system. The use of simple tools is involved in linking the pieces. The pieces are brightly colored and there is a large number of components in each kit.

Mobilo

Mobilo is a bright, durable, and easy to manipulate kit. All the parts are plastic. The wheels, hinges and turntables are simple to use and effective. They clip together easily. This kit allows the child to gain some confidence in building. Even the most inexperienced students can make working models with moving parts. Older children can make quite elaborate models.

Reo Click (Create-It)

This kit is made up of a series of tubes, rectangular plates, and wheels with a series of connectors. These connectors enable the tubes to be put together in lines or at angles to each other. This kit is extremely versatile, easy to use, strong and attractively colored. The pieces sometimes split after heavy use.

Sonos

This kit is made from brightly colored plastic pieces. The basic kit consists of square panels, supports, links, clips, different sized axles, wheels, rods, hubs, cross joints, and string. The Super Sonos also contains a variety of gears. These kits allow for the easy construction of wheeled vehicles.

Stickle Bricks

Stickle Bricks consist of squares, rectangles, triangles, and wheels which "stick" together. There are base boards and people available. Children can learn how to make a wide variety of models quickly. These kits can be combined with "straws." These kits have few problems.

Struts

This is a plastic construction set made up of flat struts which are flexible, and rigid blocks and wheels into which the struts can be slotted. They are brightly colored and durable. Immediate success is possible for the child. Simple items such as flowers and planes can be created easily. There is a motor available that can be used to make models with rotating parts. The pieces should be placed in a new container for storage.

Recommended for Grade 4-6 Students

Asmeca

This is a light, colorful, and durable kit. It consists of building pieces of various lengths with rounded ends, corner pieces, and wheels. Nuts and bolts connect the pieces. Experience is needed in the use of the tools to tighten the nuts and bolts. Students need some guidance to put together wheel and corner pieces.

Baufix

Baufix is made of wood and plastic. It is sturdy and cannot be easily damaged. It is attractively colored. The material is a type of wooden Meccano consisting of struts, cog wheels, wheels, nuts, bolts, washers and screws. Tools (hammers and screw drivers) are provided. The kit allows the children to work with nuts, bolts, and spanners.

YOUR NOTES

Capsela

Capsela consists of transparent capsules which are connected by nuts. Each capsule contains a different mechanism and by linking capsules, power can be transferred to move wheels, propellers, etc. Batteries are included in one capsule and leads link up terminals to transfer power to the motorized sections. The students can observe how simple gears work using this model. Also, it serves as an introduction to the use of batteries, axles and cogs. Some teacher guidance may be needed initially.

Fischertechnik

A durable, well-designed kit consisting of plastic construction rods of various lengths with a variety of devices to join them together. Axles, cogs, wheels, etc., are included. Various kits are available. Additional kits include motors, gears and electromechanical parts. These kits are quite expensive and if some parts are missing, it is difficult to make some of the models.

LEGO Technic

There is a wide variety of LEGO Technic kits. The basic kit forms the beginning of the LEGO Technic system. It does not contain the basic building blocks but has pieces that fit together like LEGO. These kits contain wheels, rods, struts, cogs, and hinged pieces. Work cards are included with the kits. Working models can be created. Basic construction techniques and principles can be developed through these kits. Simple gears, pulleys, levers, and machines can be worked on.

LEGO DACTA (R) Control Lab (TM)

LEGO DACTA (R) Control Lab (TM) is a control system that combines LEGO (R) elements and sensors with a special version of the Logo programming language. With Control Lab (TM), students build working models and control them using a computer. Technological concepts can be learned through open-ended design activities. In Control Lab (TM) you create and work with projects which resemble real life activities and models.

An interdisciplinary approach integrating science, technology, math, language arts, and self and society can be easily developed with this material. The LEGO DACTA (R) Control Lab (TM) system is comprised of three parts: input, process, and output. The LEGO DACTA (R) Control Lab (TM) materials, when they are connected together, make a system as shown below.

○ Input - There are three types of input into the Control Lab (TM) system. These are from the keyboard, sensors, or the mouse.

○ Process - The process component of Control Lab (TM) includes the computer, the Control Lab (TM) software, cable, and serial interface. Input into the Control Lab (TM) system is processed by the computer and the software. Instructions are communicated through the cable to the interface box.

○ Output - The output components of the Control Lab (TM) system include the motors, lamps and sound elements which are included in the LEGO DACTA (R) materials. Many different types of models can be built using LEGO (R) elements and these output devices. The output can also be on the computer screen.

LEGO DACTA (R) Serial Interface Box

The LEGO (R) models are controlled by the computer via an interface box which connects directly to the serial port of computers. There are 8 output ports for controlling motors, lamps and sound elements. There are 8 input ports for touch, temperature, angle, and light sensors.

YOUR NOTES

Planning Sheet #6 Product Evaluation K-3

Activity: _____

Student: _____

Worked with: _____

Product Type (drawing, presentation, model, working prototype): _____

Criteria	My Comments
Student understanding of problem	
Completeness of project	
Special features of note (creativity, use of materials, etc.)	
Student evaluation	
Understanding of evaluation results (Is student able to suggest improvements to design based on results?)	

Planning Sheet #7 Product Evaluation 4-6

Activity: _____

Student: _____

Worked with: _____

Product Type (drawing, presentation, model, working prototype): _____

Criteria	My Comments
Comprehension of problem	
Creativity of solution	
Drawings (complete, with labels and to scale if appropriate)	
Oral presentation (able to respond to questions?)	
Student's evaluation (was it ongoing?)	
How did student use evaluation results?	
Other	

Planning Sheet #8 Assessment (K-3)

Student Name: _____

Date: _____

Activity: _____

Observed Criteria	Ranking (1 poor to 5 excellent)
confidence	
imagination	
practical skills	
organization	
leadership	
manual dexterity	
positive attitude	
math skills	
creativity	
flexibility	
reasoning ability	
co-operation	
planning ability	
motivation	
language skills	
hand-eye co-ordination	

Planning Sheet #9 Assessment (4-6)

Student Name: _____

Date: _____

Activity: _____

Observed Criteria	Ranking (1 poor to 5 excellent)

Planning Sheet #10 For Next Time

Activity _____

What parts of this activity were most stimulating to students?

_____

_____

If any students experienced difficulty, when did this occur?

_____

_____

How well did the selected student groupings work?

_____

_____

Which materials were most suitable? Least?

_____

_____

What might you change when doing this activity again?

_____

_____

Safety Quiz

How's your safety knowledge? Have you ever worked with power tools or machinery before? Do you know what to do in an emergency? Take this quiz to help you find out.

1. Think about the equipment your teacher has shown you in the room. Where are the start and stop buttons on each piece of equipment you will be using?

2. What is dangerous about wearing the following to a class where you will be using tools?

   (a) bracelets and watches

   (b) necklaces

   (c) open-toed shoes

3. Why should you check a piece of wood for nails or other foreign materials before cutting or drilling it?

4. What should you do before changing, cleaning, or adjusting the blades on any machine?

5. Where is the nearest eye-washing station to your class? Do you know how to use it?

6. What should you do in an emergency?

7. When you should wear each of the following protections?

   (a) safety glasses

   (b) dust mask

   (c) hearing protection

   (d) apron

8. What is a push stick? When should you use one?

9. Why is it important to avoid talking to a person operating a machine?

10. If you have to leave a machine for a moment, what should you do?

11. How could you protect your fingers when using a glue gun to join two small pieces of material together?

12. If you are working on a project in a workshop, then finishing it at home or in another classroom, which safety procedures should you follow at all times?

If there is anything you were not sure about in this quiz -- or if you have any questions about the use of tools or techniques in class -- take the time to ask and find out.
It's the best way to ensure your own safety, and that of those around you.

Answers to Safety Quiz (Page 147)

The Safety Quiz will help you establish your students' understanding concerning common safety issues in technology education. Modify the Quiz to suit your needs. The Quiz and accompanying Safety Contract (page 139) should not be interpreted as a list of standards or used in place of your school's safety standards.

Quiz

1. Students should be confident about the location and use of controls, especially any safety stops, before using any machinery. Time should be invested in practicing an emergency stop.

2. (a) & (b) Jewelry and any loose objects can become caught in moving parts, causing injury. This consideration should extend to loose clothing, neckties, or scarves. (c) One of the most commonplace accidents involves the dropping of heavy and/or sharp objects. Toes should be as protected as possible.

3. The use of scrap and found materials brings with it the risk of wood that contains nails, screws, or other foreign objects. These can cause a drill bit or saw to bind and possibly snap. Also, there is the risk of metal fragments being released. Any suspect pieces of wood should be discarded.

4. The machine should be stopped, and if appropriate, the power supply disengaged.

5. Be sure students have an opportunity to see and handle the eye-washing station at your school.

6. While school policies will vary depending on the type of emergency, in general you will want students to always turn off machinery and notify the adult in charge at once.

7. (a) Safety glasses should be worn whenever machinery is being operated, dust generated, or there is a possibility of flying fragments. You may prefer to have all students wear them when fabricating is underway, if you do not have a specific work area set aside. Remember that ordinary glasses may be shatter-resistant, but they are not impact-proof and should not be used in place of proper safety glasses.
(b) Dust masks, preferably with disposable filters, should be worn whenever students producing fine dust, such as during sanding, as well as when they apply finishes. Consult your school safety standards for guidance.

(c) As a rule of thumb, ear protection is needed whenever the level of noise is such that you cannot clearly hear a person speaking normally from a distance of 1 m. Consult your school safety standards for guidelines.
(d) Protective aprons are recommended when students are doing metal-work. Consult your school safety standards for guidance.

8. A push stick is a piece of scrap wood or plastic that is used instead of the hands to manipulate materials into the cutting edge of a saw or other machine. As a guideline, a push stick should be used within 10 cm of any blade, and whenever a push needs to be applied directly in the cutting path.

9. A machine operator should never be distracted by conversation or people moving around nearby. Otherwise, an accident or mistake could result.

10. Before being left unattended, machinery must always be turned off.

11. Answers will vary. For example, using pliers to hold the objects. The point is to remind students that there is a risk of minor burn from any hot glue and they should use it with caution.

12. This question is to address the problem of having students working in several different areas, including the possibility of some work being done at home. Ideally, students should follow the safety procedures given to them by the specialist in the use of the equipment, whether a technology education teacher, supervisor, or invited guest expert. You will have to ensure that every teacher the student encounters in a project will be using the same standards. It is also highly recommended that students receive a written set of safety standards that they must carry with them throughout the work.

Safety Contract

I have read and understood all of the following principles of safe practice in this class. I know that it is my responsibility to follow the safety standards set by my teacher. I know that is my school's and my teacher's responsibility to set these standards in order to make a safe workplace for myself and my fellow students. I will ask if I am unsure at any time about the safe use of tools, material, or equipment.

The Principles of Safe Practice

1. I will bring to the class a positive attitude about personal and group safety.
2. I will make sure that I am appropriately dressed when I will be using tools or other equipment in the classroom, including the use of safety glasses and aprons when necessary.
3. I am aware of potential safety hazards at home and in the workplace.
4. I know the school and classroom safety procedures.
5. I know what to do in case of an accident or other emergency.
6. I know and use safe work habits.
7. I am committed to keeping the work areas properly maintained, including proper clean up and care of equipment.
8. When I am using specialized technological equipment, such as in a technology education workshop or other facility, I will follow the safe-use instructions provided by the teacher in charge of that equipment.
9. I will notify my teacher promptly of any problems with equipment or other potential safety hazards.

Together we will work safely.

STUDENT'S SIGNATURE _____ DATE _____

TEACHER'S SIGNATURE _____

Evaluation Form (K-3)

Activity: _____

Student's Name: _____

The problem was: _____

_____

My design helps by:

I could make my design better by:

Next time, I would like to: _____

_____

Evaluation Form (4-6)

Activity: _____

Student's Name: _____

Worked with: _____

The Problem: _____

_____

What factors were important to consider when solving the problem?

_____

_____

_____

How my design helped to solve the problem:

Describe how well you think your device would do its job.

_____

_____

What do you like the best about your device?

_____

_____

If you made this device again, what would you change or improve?

_____

_____

Self-assessment Form (K-3)

Name: _____

This is how I feel about my project.

Self-assessment Form (4-6)

Activity: _____

Name: _____

Circle the number that best describes your work. Think of it as a way of remembering how the project went and what you might do differently next time.

  5   excellent
  4   very good
  3   good
  2   satisfactory
  1   poor

Effort

I tried as hard as I could.	1	2	3	4	5
I looked for help when I needed it.	1	2	3	4	5
I helped others in my group.	1	2	3	4	5

Investigating

I used books and other references.	1	2	3	4	5
I talked to people.	1	2	3	4	5
I used a computer search.	1	2	3	4	5

Construction

I contributed to the work.	1	2	3	4	5
I listened to others.	1	2	3	4	5
I had a task of my own.	1	2	3	4	5

Time

I did not waste my time.	1	2	3	4	5
I did not waste anyone else's time.	1	2	3	4	5
I finished on time.	1	2	3	4	5

Choose one item from the ones above in which you think you could improve. What would you do differently next time? _____

_____

Peer Assessment Form (4-6)

Activity: _____

Name of student being assessed: _____

Circle the number that best describes the student's work on the activity just completed.
Try to be fair and honest.

5	excellent
4	very good
3	good
2	satisfactory
1	poor

Effort

Concentrated on the task.	1 2 3 4 5
Looked for help when I needed it.	1 2 3 4 5
Helped others in the group.	1 2 3 4 5

Investigating

Used books and other references.	1 2 3 4 5
Contacted people.	1 2 3 4 5
Used a computer search.	1 2 3 4 5

Construction

Contributed to the work.	1 2 3 4 5
Listened to others.	1 2 3 4 5
Took responsibility for a task.	1 2 3 4 5

Time

Did not waste my time.	1 2 3 4 5
Did not waste anyone else's time.	1 2 3 4 5
Finished on time.	1 2 3 4 5

Choose one item from the ones above in which you think this student could improve.
Suggest what the student might do differently next time._____

Group Assessment Form (4-6)

Activity: _____

Team Members: _____

Agree on your answers as a group. Circle your choice.

1. Did we share?	yes	sometimes	no
2. Did we take turns?	yes	sometimes	no
3. Did everyone contribute?	yes	sometimes	no
4. Did we listen to each other?	yes	sometimes	no
5. Did we help each other?	yes	sometimes	no

Finish each sentence.

6. We agreed on _____

_____

7. We disagreed on _____

_____

We each had a task. The tasks were:

_____

_____

_____

9. We could improve by

_____

Glossary

Aesthetics - the characteristics of an object or system that appeals to the sense of beauty.

Bending - If a force is applied to the centre of a structure such as a plank, it will bend in the middle as the force is increased. The material has to be rigid enough to resist the force and therefore not bend. If a force is applied at the end of a structure, without support, bending will occur at that end.

Cellular Forms - the combining of several tubes to produce a structure that is effective at resisting pressure applied to the ends of the tube, i.e. compression.

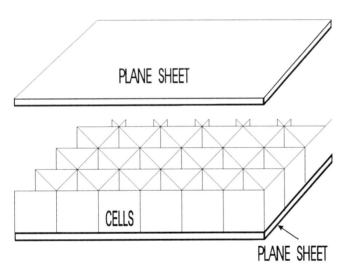

PLANE SHEET

CELLS

PLANE SHEET

Compression - where a load tends to squash an object, such as when a person leans on the back of a chair.

Control - the means by which mechanisms are regulated.

Corrigation - the repeated folding of material to provide rigidity at right angles to the folds and flexibility in the direction of the folds.

Demand - characteristics or features that must be addressed in the design solution. For example, safety is a demand. (Engineering terminology refers to demands as specifications.)

Design - a proposed solution to a problem.

Design brief - a statement of the problem, giving demands and preferences.

Device - something designed to serve a particular function.

Efficient - able to do something with little waste of time or energy.

Effort - a force applied to a machine to produce an action.

Ergonomics - the efficiency of an object or system in relation to the work performed by the human body and mind in using it.

Evaluation - how well the design meets the essential demands and preferences.

Exploded view - a drawing that shows an object as if pulled apart, giving details of all of the parts the object and how the parts fit together.

Fabrication - the act or process of forming and assembling materials and structures.

Finishing - the final stages of smoothing, painting, staining, and applying protective coatings to a project. Done both to enhance appearance and to protect the object from the environment.

Function - the use(s) to which an object or system is put.

Isometric drawing - a method of drawing that produces a three-dimensional view of an object. All vertical lines remain at 90° to the horizontal and all others are drawn at 30° to the horizontal. Isometric grid paper is recommended.

Interaction - the way that component parts act on each other or with each other.

Machine - a mechanism or device that helps people do work. The main machines are the lever, the pulley, the wheel and axle, and the inclined plane (wedge and screw).

Materials - the substance from which a structure is made.

Mechanism - the parts of structure that allow it to work or function.

Miter (mitre) box - a box used to hold a backsaw in a locked vertical position and while the cut is made in a piece of wood at a desired angle.

Model- typically a preliminary construction of some or all of a design, made from simple materials such as clay or paper, that can be used to test the design's features.

Modem - a device that connects one computer to another over a telephone line.

Orthographic drawing - a method of drawing the true shape of the surfaces of three-dimensional objects. Each surface is drawn separately as though being faced by the observer. Grid paper is recommended.

Power/energy - the resource that enables a mechanism to perform work.

Preference - any optional characteristics or factors that would be preferred in the solution to a problem. For example, a personal choice as to type of finish.

Prototype - the first practical try-out of anything. The original or model version.

Shear - where loads push at right angles to the surface of an object, such as when scissors are used to cut paper.

Spreadsheet - a piece of computer software that allows for the manipulation and display of numerical data.

Strut - The parts that have to resist compressive forces are called struts.

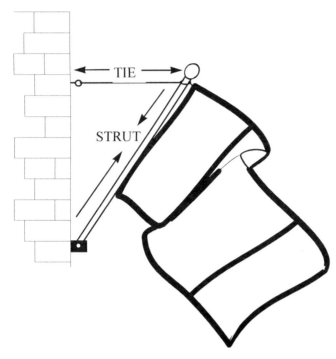

Structure - the essential physical or conceptual parts of buildings, etc. and the way in which they are constructed or organized.

System - comprehensive, self-sustaining combinations of interrelated structures, mechanisms, etc.

Technology - the use of knowledge or the practical means people use to change their surroundings.

Tension - where a load tends to pull or stretch an object apart, such as when two people pull on a rope. (In building construction, the parts that are in tension are call ties.)

Tie - in structural work, the parts that are in tension are called ties (ties are usually thinner than parts that have to resist compressive forces.)

Torsion - where a load tends to twist an object, such as when a person tightens the handle of a vice clamp.

Triangulation - where a triangular form is made in order to provide a strong rigid shape. For example, adding a strut made from card diagonally from one corner to another in a square shape, divides the square into two triangles which add strength.

USEFUL RESOURCES

For Students in Grades K-3

Adkins, J. *How a House Happens*, Walker and Co., ISBN# 0-8027-7206-4

Barton, B. *Building a House*, Mulberry, ISBN# 0-688-09356-6

Cobb, V. & J. Strejan, *A Pop-Up Book Skyscraper Going Up*, Crowell, ISBN# 0-690-04525-5

Duncan, M. *How Is It Made — Skyscrapers*, Faber & Faber Ltd., ISBN # 0-571-14730-5

Gibbons, G. *New Road*, Harper & Row, ISBN# 0-06-446059-2

Gibbons, G. *Trucks*, Harper & Row, ISBN# 0-06-443069-3

Gibbons, G. *Up Goes the Skyscraper!*, Macmillan Publishing Co., ISBN# 0-689-71411-4

Ingoglia, G. *The Big Book of Real Skyscrapers*, Grosset & Dunlap, ISBN# 0-448-19186-5

Little, K., *Things On Wheels*, Usborne Publishing Ltd., ISBN# 1-85123191-9

Osborne, V., Rex, *The Most Special Car in the World*, Pan Books, ISBN# 0-330-31313-4

Peppe, R., *The Mice and the Clockwork Bus*, Puffin, ISBN #0-14-050613-6

Royston, A. & G. Thompson, *Monster Building Machines*, Barrons, ISBN# 0-8120-6174-8

Steltzer, U., *Building an Igloo*, Groundwood, ISBN# 0-88899-118-5

Strickland, P., *Machines As Big As Monsters*, Kids Can Press, ISBN# 0-921103-72-7

Strickland P., *Machines As Big As Giants*, Kids Can Press, ISBN# 0-921103-74-3

Wagner, J., *The Machine at the Heart of the World*, Kestrell Books, ISBN 0-7226-64826

Weiss, H., *Shelters From Tepee to Igloo*, Thomas Y. Crowell, N.Y., ISBN: 0-690-04553-0

YOUR NOTES

For Students in Grades 3-6

The Way Things Work, Macaulay, David, Houghton Mifflin Co., Boston, Mass. (also available on CD-ROM)

Williams, J., *Flight*, Wayland, ISBN# 0-7502-0026-X

Williams, J., *Machines*, Wayland, ISBN# 0-7502-0025-1

Wilson, F., *What it Feels Like to be a Building*, Doubleday and Co., ISBN# 0-89133-142-5

Wyler, R., *Science Fun With Toy Cars and Trucks*, Messner, ISBN# 0-671-65854-9

Zubrowski, B., *Wheels At Work*, Wm. Morrow, ISBN# 0-688-06349-7

(Other good resources by Bernie Zubrowski in the Boston Children's Museum Activity series are also available, including *Structures, Clocks, and Raceways*)

Useful Teacher Resources

Good ideas to assist teachers with the design process:

Collins Technology for Key Stage 3: Design and Technology, the Process. Chapman, C., et al. 1992, London: Collins Educational.

Good ideas for projects for elementary students:

Technology I.D.E.A.S., Corney, Bob & Dale, Norman, 1993, Maxwell MacMillan Canada, ISBN 0-02-954154-9.

Good project ideas:

Technology: Science & Math in Action Book 1, ISBN 0-02-636945-1; *Technology: Science & Math in Action Book 2*, ISBN 0-02-636948-6, Glencoe, McGraw Hill, New York, 1995.

Living with Technology, Hacker & Borden, Nelson Canada, Scarborough, ISBN 0-8273-4907-6.

Technology Science and Mathematics; Connection Activities: A Teachers Resource Binder, (Correlated to *Technology: Science & Math in Action Books*), La Porte, McGraw Hill, 1996.

Instead of a nature walk, take your students on a technowalk (or several of them). The book gives ideas on how to do it:

Take a TechnoWalk, Williams, Peter & Jacobson, Saryl, Trifolium Books Inc., Toronto, Ontario, in development, ISBN 1-895579-76-6.

Excellent ideas on science teaching and a good section on integration with mathematics and technology:

Measuring Up: Prototypes for Mathematics Assessment. Mathematical Sciences Education Board, National Research Council. Washington, DC: National Academy Press, 1993

National Science Education Standards. Washington, DC: National Academy Press, ISBN 0-309-05326-9

The Ultimate Teacher Resource on Using the Internet!

The book has wonderful features for teachers — "Getting Started" exercises encourage teachers to explore Internet use for themselves, and "Project Ideas" provide many, many ideas for student use at all levels, from K-12. And at the end of the book — a bonus — an appendix of great educational resources that can be found on the Internet.

The Teacher's Complete & Easy Guide to the Internet, Heide, Ann & Stilborne, Linda, 1996 Trifolium Books Inc., Toronto, Ontario, ISBN 1-895579-85-6.

YOUR NOTES

YOUR NOTES

Internet Sites: Connecting on your own

Netscape is presently the best Web software to enable you to contact a wealth of resources on the World Wide Web. Please observe your own school's security policies, before you assign students to get into the Internet. Once in Netscape, you will see a number of "search engines," additional pieces of software, embedded in Netscape, which will let you search for any and every topic you can imagine. Some of the search engines include "Web Crawler," and "Yahoo." Once underway, simply type in your topic, sit back and wait for the computers to talk to one another. This, in turn, will usually give rise to a number of resources and links to other sites and resources. Be forewarned: surfing the net can be addictive. Doing it on a school night might make it difficult to get to class the next morning![1]

There is a Yahoo search page specifically of interest to K-12 students and teachers. It, like the main Yahoo search engine, allows users to search for information using the keywords supplied by the user, but this specific page allows the search to be confined to things that might be of interest to educators and students.[2]

http://beta.yahoo.com/Education/K_12

The following web site, posted by *Discover Magazine,* is full of links to other science and technology related sites. Although this site is not intended for younger students, it is an excellent starting point for your research and for older students.

http://www.enews.com:80/magazines/discover/

Addresses about Space and Technology

The following two web sites contain accounts of projects by students building Mars robots.

http://www.lunacorp.com/lcrover.htm

http://esther.la.asu.edu/asu_tes/TES_Editor/TESNEWS/4_VOL/No_2/re

Educational Space Simulations Project. Includes: Space simulation "starter kit" for educators, student activities and experiments for use in space, launch and landing scripts.[3]

http://chico.rice.edu/armadillo/Simulations/simserver.html

Arizona Mars K-12 Education Program - brings Mars into the classroom with reading lists, missions, Mars facts and teacher's resources. Includes useful links such as: "Educational Resources at other WWW sites" "Planetary Science and Space Internet Links"[3]

http://esther.la.asu.edu/asu_tes/TES_Editor/educ_activities_info.html

Canadian space information: meet Canada's latest astronauts! [3]

http://schoolnet2.carleton.ca/english/astronauts/astronauts.html

Space Telescope Electronic Information Service Home Page. A wide array of information and educational resources. See the "Public" section for support materials for teachers.[3]

http://marvel.stsci.edu/top.html

Sites about Math

MathPro: puzzles, problems and resources[3]

http://sashimi.wwa.com:80/math/

The MegaMath Glossary and Reference Section. [3]

http://www.c3.lanl.gov/mega-math/gloss/gloss.html

Fun Math Things. Includes: paradoxes and logic puzzles. [3]

http://www.uni.uiuc.edu/departments/math/glazer/fun_math.html

Other Sites of Interest

A learning kit of activities and lesson plans focused on motion.[3]

http://schoolnet2.carleton.ca/english/worldinmotion/index.html

Elementary and Junior High. A young student describes 3 successful projects that could be used as activities. Erosion, Battery Power, Soil Pollution. [3]

http://megamach.portage.net:80/~bgidzak/nick.html

Australia: A girls' science and technology high school has a webpage with links to some of their own experiments and projects in robotics and other things.[2]

http://www.ozemail.com.au/~mghslib/projects/mghsproj.html

An American webpage similar to the Australian one, above, that has good ideas, can be found at this address.[2]

http://forum.swarthmore.edu/sum95/projects.html

[1] Thanks to Professor Don Galbraith for allowing us to use his introduction to Netscape here (adapted from *A Portfolio of Teaching Ideas for High School Biology*, Trifolium Books Inc.)
[2] Thanks to John Rising for locating sites he thought would be of special interest.
[3] Thanks to Ann Heide and Linda Stilborne, *The Teacher's Complete & Easy Guide to the Internet* for allowing us to include a few of the many sites they have identified.

Some Suppliers

Locally available materials are adequate for most projects. For some projects you may find the following addresses useful for kit supplies and other materials. Lasy, Fischertechnik, and Lego Technic kits are available from several of the following addresses.

Canada

B. & B. School supplies
75 Watline Avenue
Mississauga, ON, L4Z 3E3
1-800-668-1108
Tel. (905) 890-0404

Boreal Laboratories Ltd.
399 Vansickle Road
St. Catharines, ON, L2S 3T4
1-800-387-9393
Tel. (416) 984-3000
Fax (416) 984-3311

Edmund Scientific Products
3350 Dufferin Street
Toronto, ON, M6A 3A4
Tel . (416) 787-4582
Fax (416) 787-5140

Efstons Scientific Suppliers Inc.
3350 Dufferin Street
Toronto, ON, M6A 3A4
Tel . (416) 787-4581 or 787-4584
Fax (416) 787-5140

Exclusive Educational Games of Excellence Inc.
243 Saunders Road
Barrie, ON, L4M 6E7
1-800-563-1166
Tel. (705) 725-1166
Fax (705) 725-1167

Gerrielle's
28-3265 South Millway
Mississauga, ON, L5L 2R3
Tel. (905) 828-4242

Lasy Canada, Ltd./Ltée
108 Lake Erie Place S.E.
Calgary, AB, T2J 2L4
Tel. (403) 271-7657
Fax (403) 278-4863

Louise Kool & Galt Limited
180 Middlefield Road
Scarborough, ON, M1S 4M6
1-800-268-4011
Tel. (416) 293-0312
Fax (416) 293-9543

The Science Source
[LINX is a trademark of The Science Source]
P.O. Box 727
Waldoboro, Maine, 04572
1-800-299-LINX
Tel. (207) 832-6344
Fax (207) 832-7281

Spectrum Educational Supplies Ltd.
125 Mary Street
Aurora, ON, L4G 1G3
Tel. (905) 841-0600
Toronto line: (905) 773-0600
Fax (905) 727-6265

Technology Teaching Systems
45 Basaltic Drive, Unit 2
Concord, ON, L4K 1G5
1-800-265-3847
Tel. (905) 660-3933 call Steve Rogers

United States

Creative Learning Systems, Inc.
16510 Via Esprillo
San Diego, CA 92127-1708
1-800-458-2880
Fax (619) 675-7707

IASCO
5724 West 36th Street
Minneapolis, MN 55416-2594
1-800-328-4827
Lasy U.S.A. Ltd.
1309 Webster Avenue
Fort Collins, Colorado 80524
1-800-444-2126

Michigan Products Incorporated (MPI)
1200 Keystone Avenue
P.O. 24155
Lansing, Michigan
48909-4155
Tel. (517) 393-0440
Fax (517) 393-8884

PASCO Scientific
10101 Foothills Boulevard
P.O. Box 619011
Roseville, CA 95678-9011
1-800-772-8700

Pitsco
P.O. Box 1328
Pittsburg, KS 66762
1-800-842-0581

Science Kit
777 East Park Drive
Tonawanda, New York 14150
Tel. (716) 874-6020
Fax (716) 874-9572

The Science Source
[LINX is a trademark of The Science Source]
P.O. Box 727
Waldoboro, Maine, 04572
1-800-299-LINX
Tel. (207) 832-6344
Fax (207) 832-7281

YOUR NOTES

More About Trifolium Titles

If you wish further information about any of these titles, please contact:

Trifolium Books Inc.
238 Davenport Road,
Suite 28
Toronto, Ontario
M5R 1J6

Tel: (416) 925-0765
Fax: 416-485-5563
E-mail: trising@io.org

Or check out our website:

www.pubcouncil.ca/trifolium

Trifolium Books Inc. is a publishing house that specializes in teacher and student resources. One of its mandates is to search out and publish exemplary materials produced by teachers. It is Trifolium's hope that you will find some or all of the following resources helpful in your classroom.

Science, Mathematics, and Technology

By Design, Technology Exploration & Integration, The Metropolitan Toronto School Board (Problem-solving through design and technology. Activities and teacher support, Grades 6-9)

Mathematics, Science, & Technology Connections, Peel Board of Education Teachers (Cross-curricular activities and planning assistance, Grades 6-9)

A Portfolio of Teaching Ideas for High School Biology, edited by Galbraith, Don (New activities and ideas, Grades 9-12)

Career and Guidance

Career Connections Series, (Trifolium Books Inc./Weigl Educational Publishers) Career exploration integrated with activities in math, science, technology and other subject areas; each book contains interviews with 10 people. (Grades 6-9)

Series I:

Great Careers for People Interested in Living Things, Czerneda, Julie

Great Careers for People Interested in the Human Body, Edwards, Lois

Great Careers for People Concerned About the Environment, Grant, Lesley

Great Careers for People Who Like Being Outdoors, Mason, Helen

Great Careers for People Interested in How Things Work, Richardson, Peter & Richardson, Bob

Great Careers for People Interested in Math & Computers, Richardson, Peter & Richardson, Bob

Teacher Resource Bank Series I, Czerneda, Julie & Studd, David

Series II:

Great Careers for People Interested in the Performing Arts, Bartlett, Gillian

Great Careers for People Who Like to Work with Their Hands, Czerneda, Julie

Great Careers for People Interested in Sports & Fitness, Edwards, Lois

Great Careers for People Who Want to Be Entrepreneurs, Lang, Jim

Great Careers for People Who Like Working with People, Mason, Helen

Great Careers for People Interested in Film, Video, & Photography, Rising, David

Teacher Resource Bank Series II, Czerneda, Julie & Toffolo, Caroline

Series III:

Great Careers for People Interested in Art & Design, Bartlett, Gillian

Great Careers for People Interested in Communications Technology, Czerneda, Julie & Vincent, Victoria

Great Careers for People Interested in Food, Mason, Helen

Great Careers for People Interested in the Past, Vincent, Victoria

Great Careers for People Fascinated by Government & Law, Males, Anne Marie, Czerneda, Julie, & Vincent, Victoria

Great Careers for People Interested in Travel & Tourism, Sharon, Donna & Sommers, Jo Anne

Teacher Resource Bank Series III, Czerneda, Julie & Baker-Proud, Susan

(For Grades 9-12)

The BreakAway Company, Campbell, Don, Pharand, Gisele, Serff, Pamela, & Williams, David (An employment skills program for students in difficulty.)

CareerWorld, Freeman, John & Balanchuk, Mary (Career-readiness program promoting equity.)

WonderTech Work Skills Simulation, Woodward, Brian & Cairns, Kathleen (Complete kit to engage a class in a realistic, hands-on, manufacturing company scenario.)

Stay in Control: The Real Key to Job-Hunting Success, Andrade, Carla-Krystin (A practical guide for handling stress to get that job.)

Make Your Own Breaks: Become and Entrepreneur & Create Your Own Future, Lang Jim (Activity-driven and full of case studies of successful entrepreneurs.)

Professional Resources

The following practical, teacher-tested guides can help you be successful using technology, make the most of your resources, and gain valuable professional development.

The Teacher's Complete and Easy Guide to the Internet, Heide, Ann & Stilborne, Linda (Comprehensive and educator-specific resource, with activities, tested Internet addresses, and more.)

The Technological Classroom: A Blueprint for Success, Heide, Ann & Henderson, Dale (A practical guide to integrating technology in all educational settings, from floor plans to strategies for active learning.)

Why the Information Highway? Lessons from Open & Distance Learning, edited by Roberts, Judith & Keough, Erin (Practical applications supported by pertinent theory and analysis, presented by colleagues established in the use of the latest technologies.)

Feeling As a Way of Knowing, Artz, Sibylle (Of value in particular for individuals working as counsellors, in child care, in social work, and psychology.)

Dear Reader,

Has this book "worked" for you? We hope you have enjoyed using the ideas in *All Aboard! Cross-Curricular Design and Technology Strategies and Activities*, and feel that by using these ideas in your classroom, you have enhanced your students' problem-solving skills <u>and</u> desire to learn. We are pleased to have the opportunity to make this book available to you, and we hope you will find other resources in our ***Springboards for Teaching*** series, as well as Trifolium's other educational resources, of great value both to your students and for your own learning.

None of us are immune to the praise and criticism of others, and those of us who write, edit, and publish educational resources such as this one are no different. Please let us hear from you about, yes, both your criticism and your praise. We need to know what you find useful about each of our resrouces and what you would like to see developed differently. We are committed to producing exemplary resources that are truly useful to you. Thus, if you have any comments or recommendations that you feel would assist us in the development of future projects and perhaps a new edition of *All Aboard!* in the future, we welcome them. Please write, fax, or e-mail Trifolium at your convenience.

Do you have a project idea that you think other teachers would find helpful? If so, please send it to us for consideration. Our aim is to continue providing practical, effective educational resources, particularly in the areas of mathematics, science, and technology, and also in career development.

We look forward to hearing from you with your thoughts about this book, new project ideas, or both!

Yours sincerely,

Trudy L. Rising
President
Trifolium Books Inc.
238 Davenport Road, Suite 28
Toronto, Ontario M5R 1J6
fax 416-485-5563
www.pubcouncil.ca/trifolium